CAREFREE

&

RETRO

COLORING BOOK

BROOKS BROTHERZ

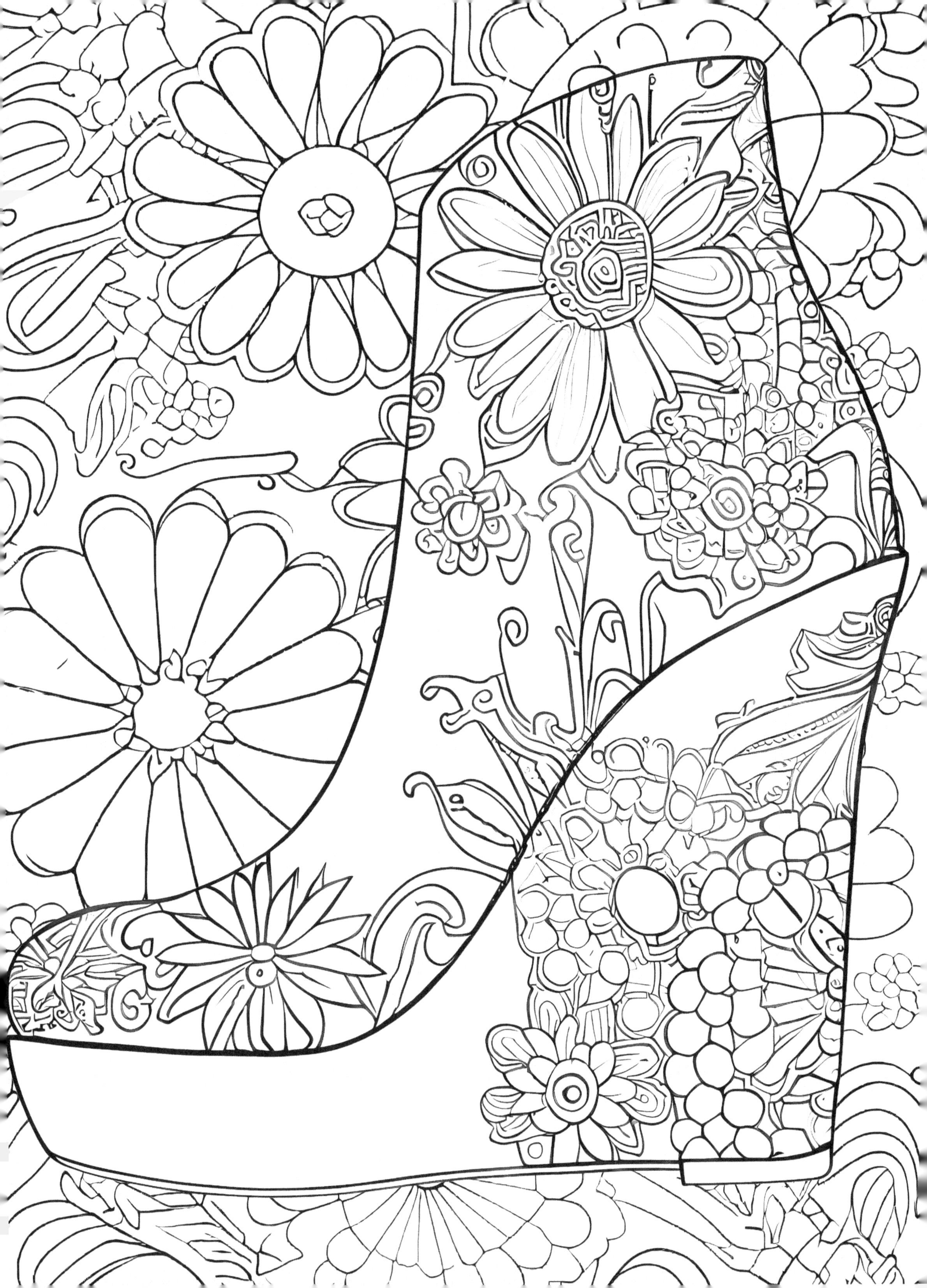

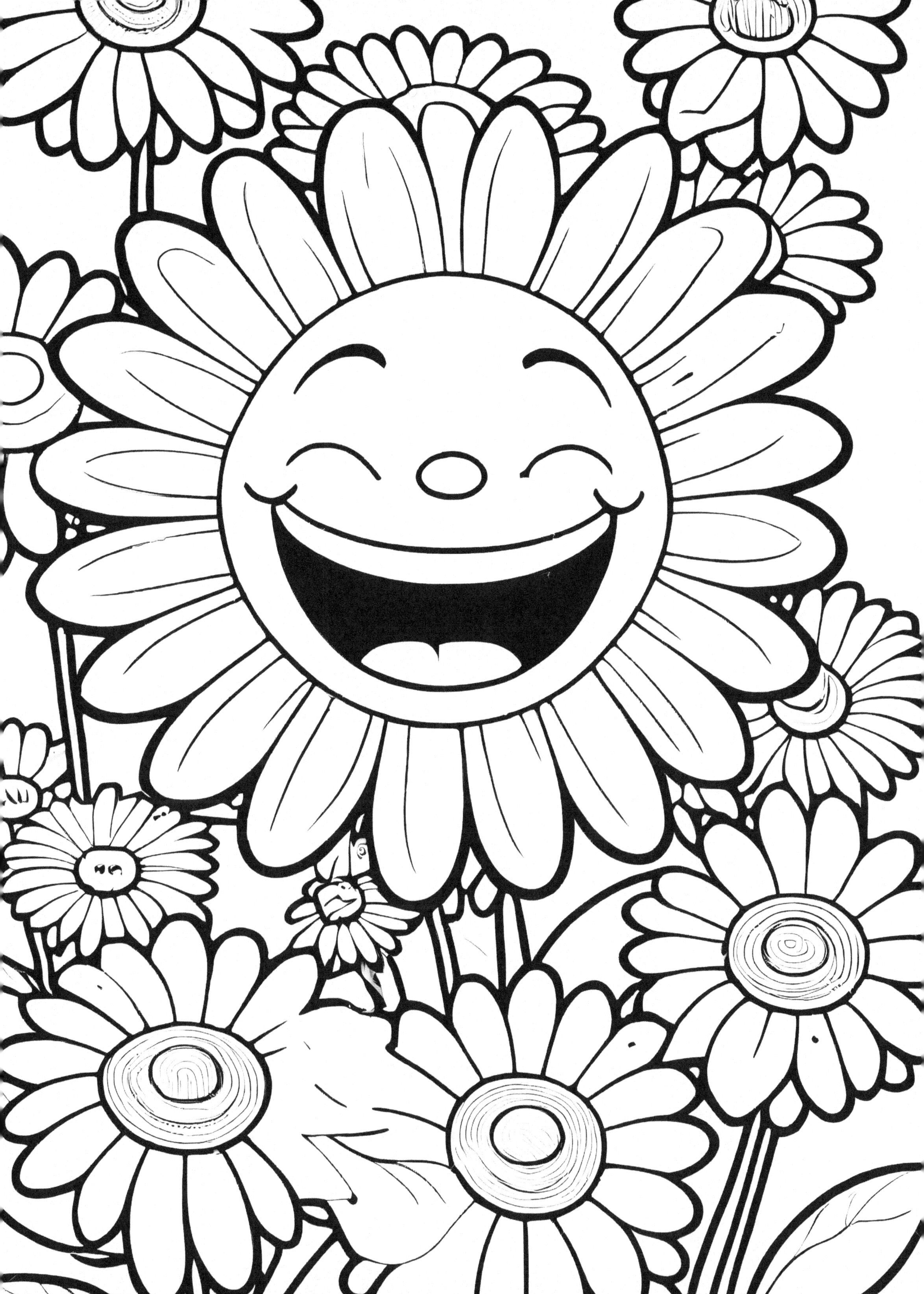

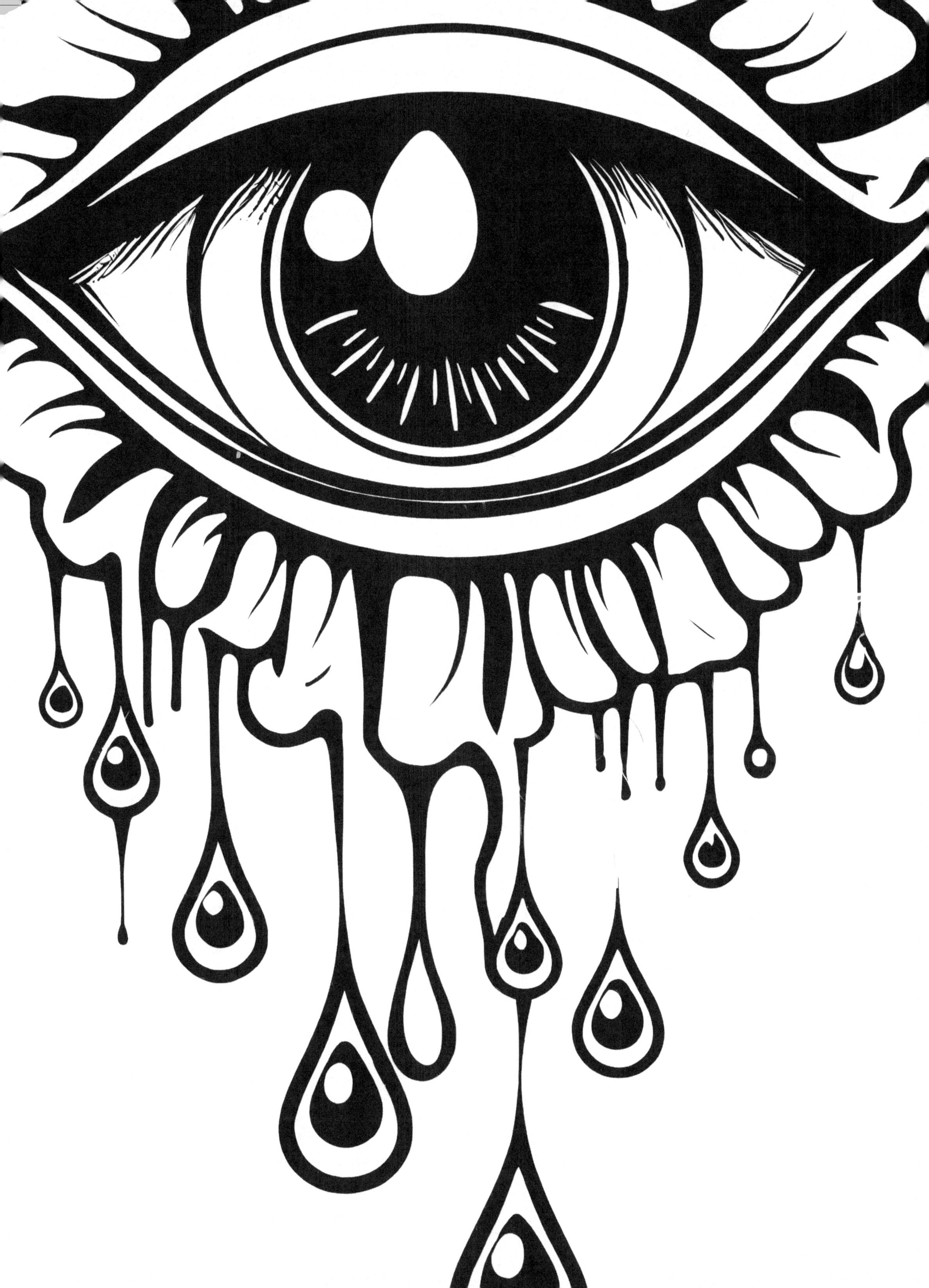

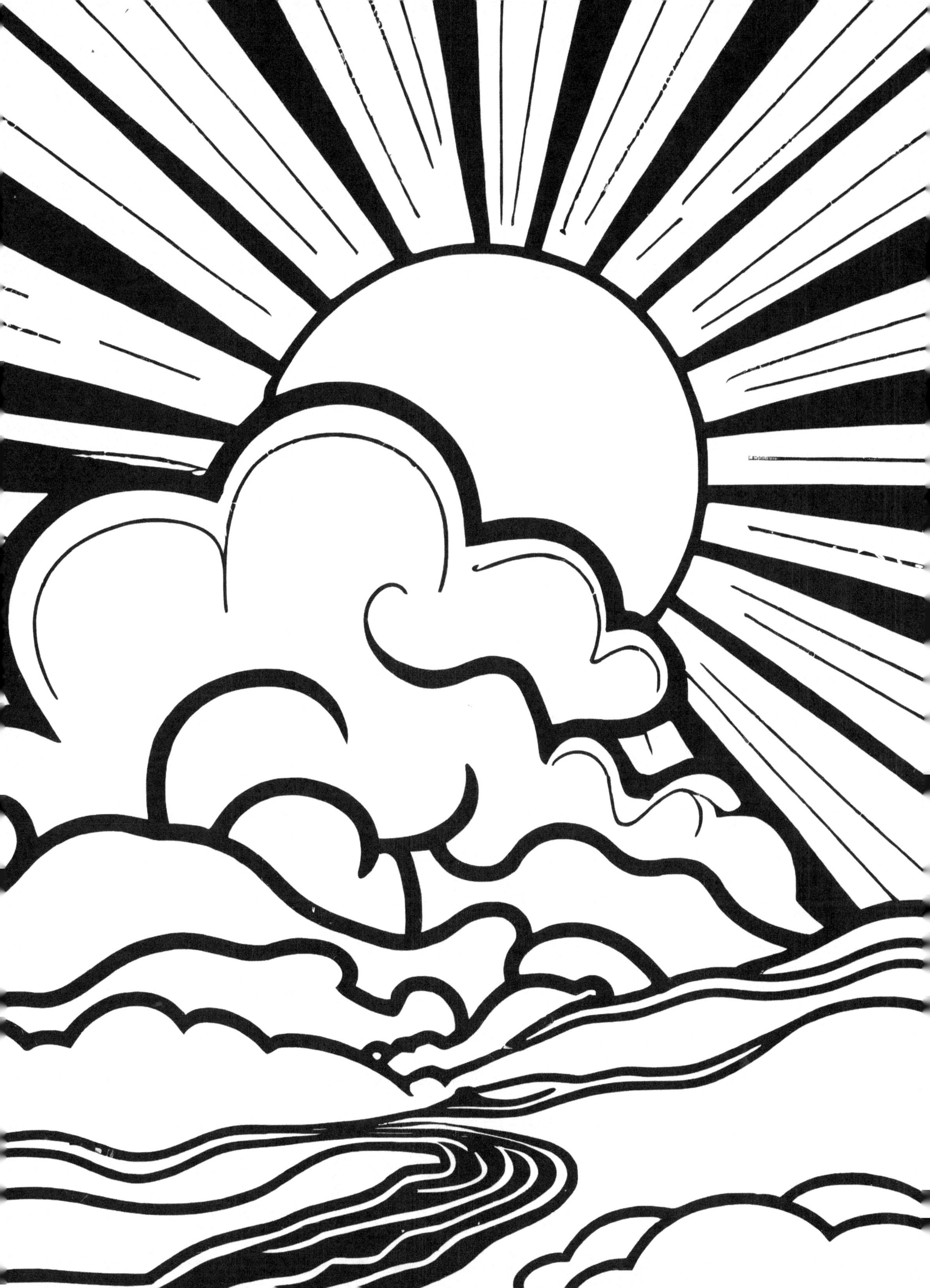

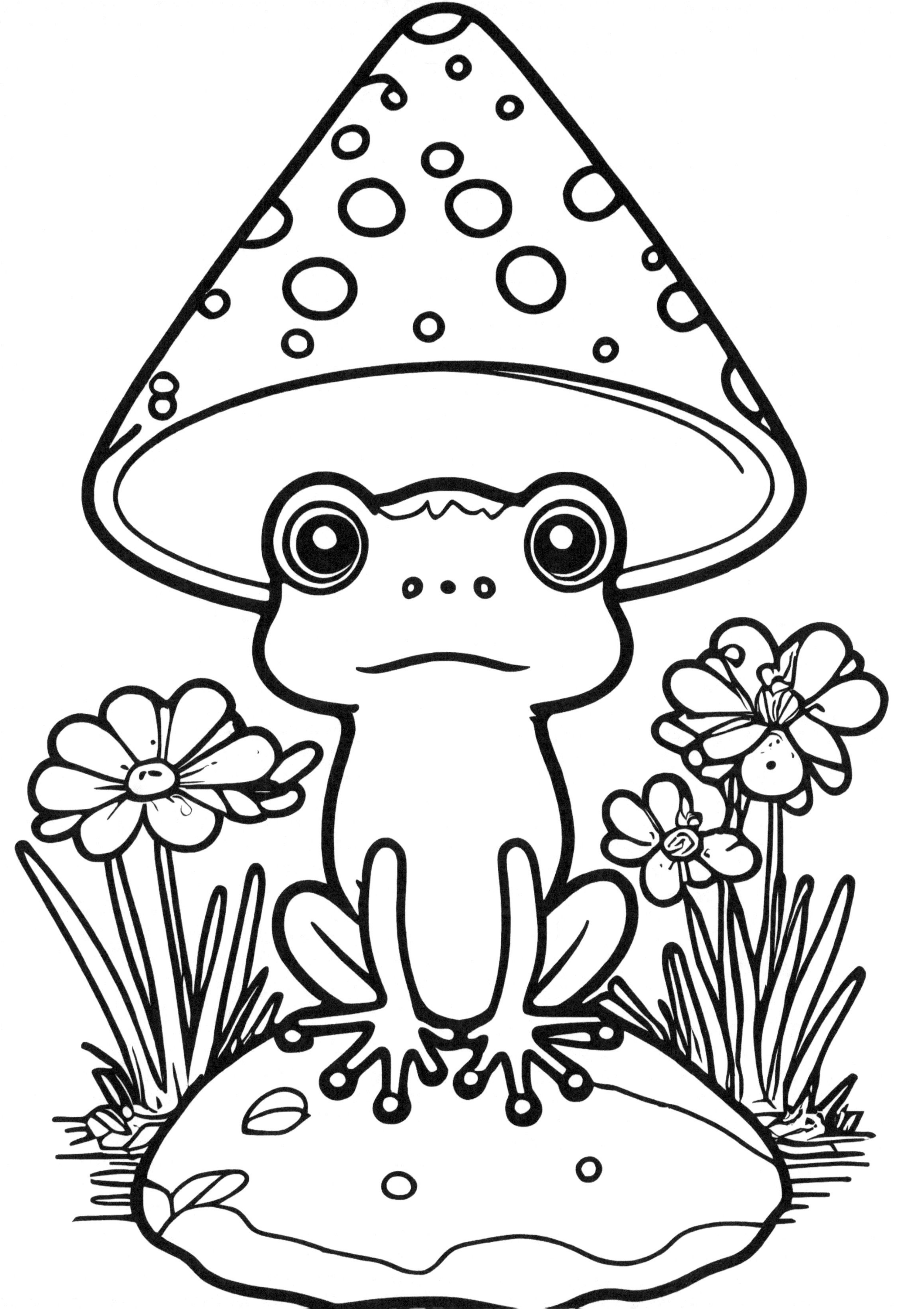

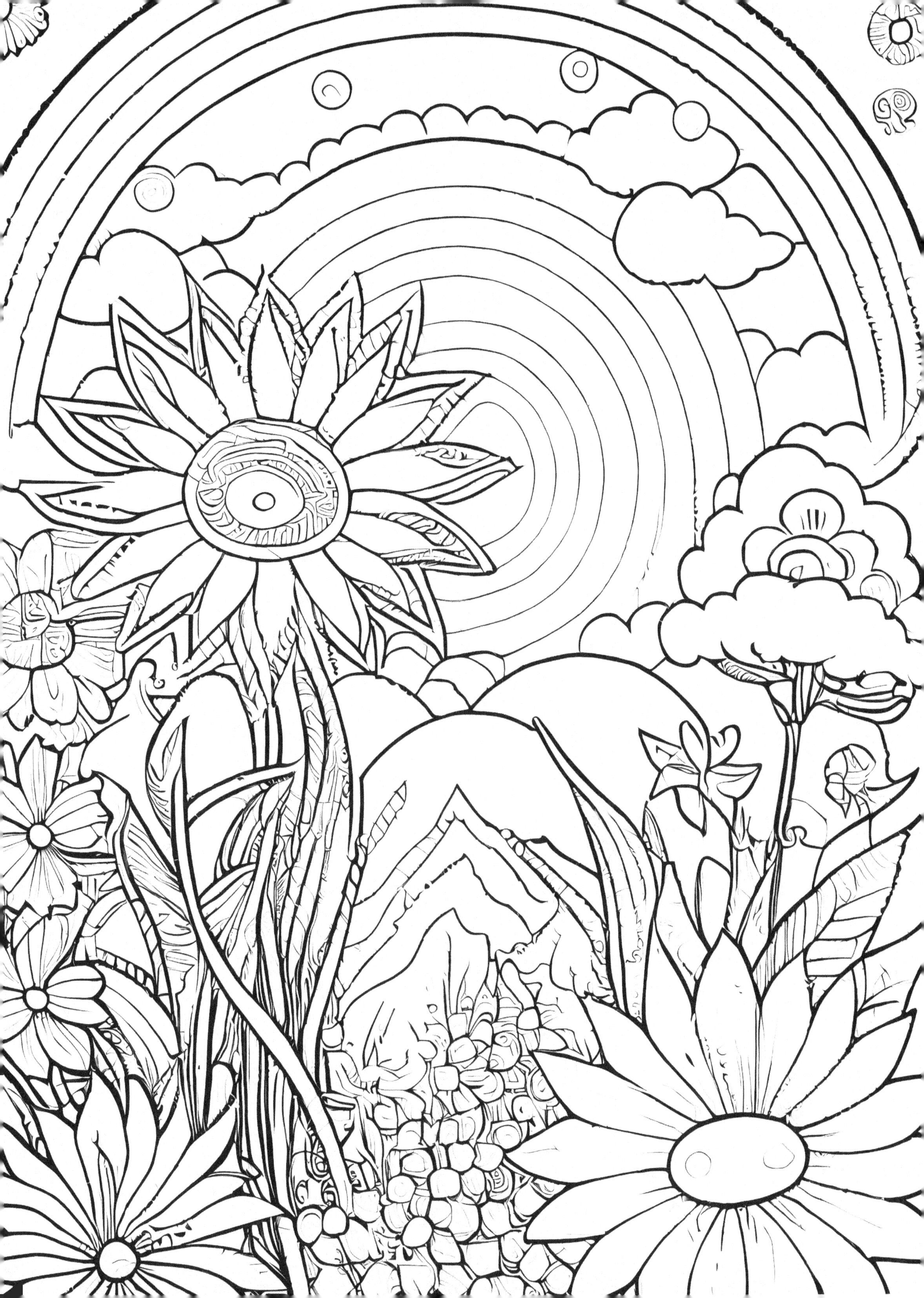

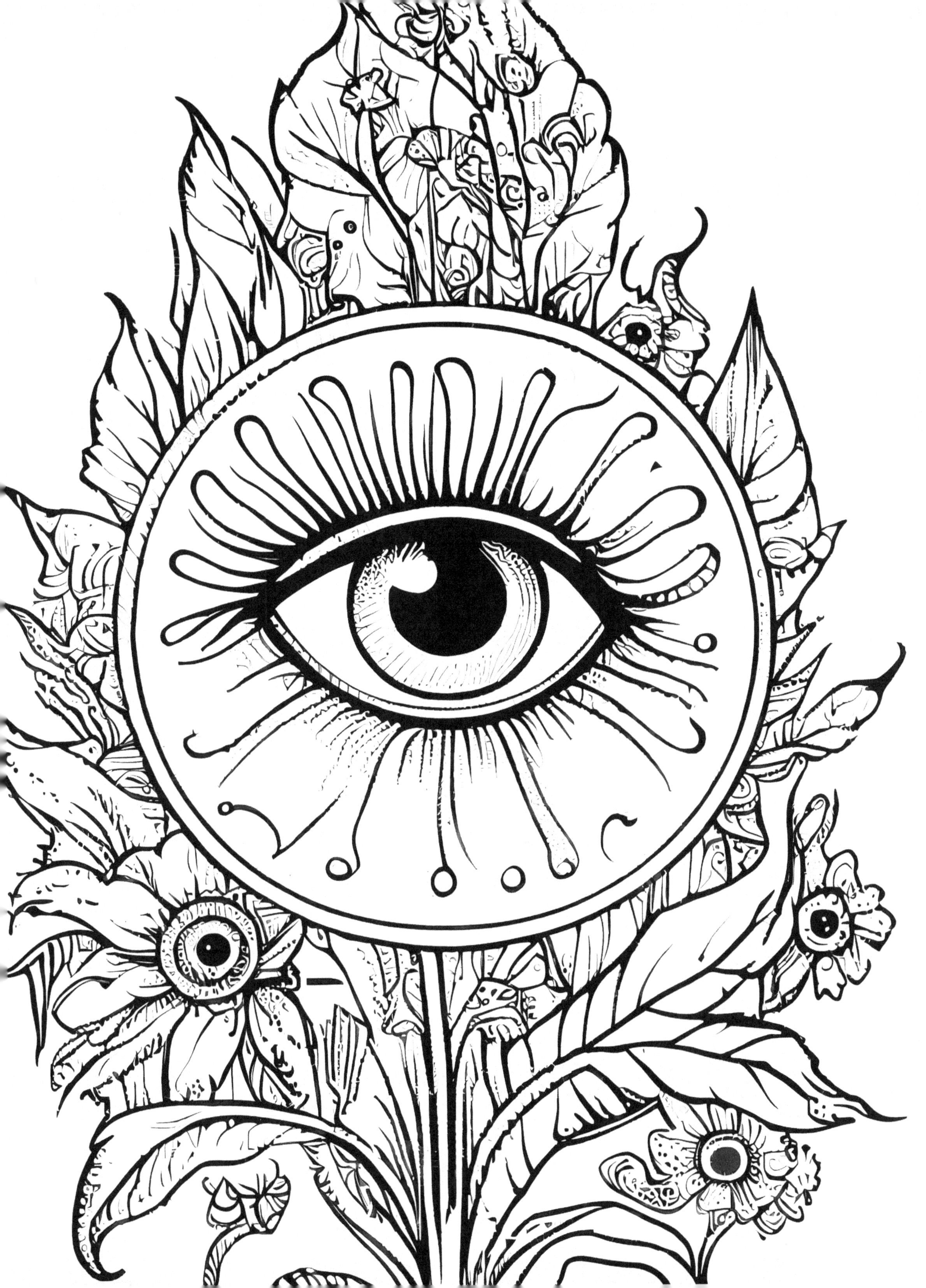

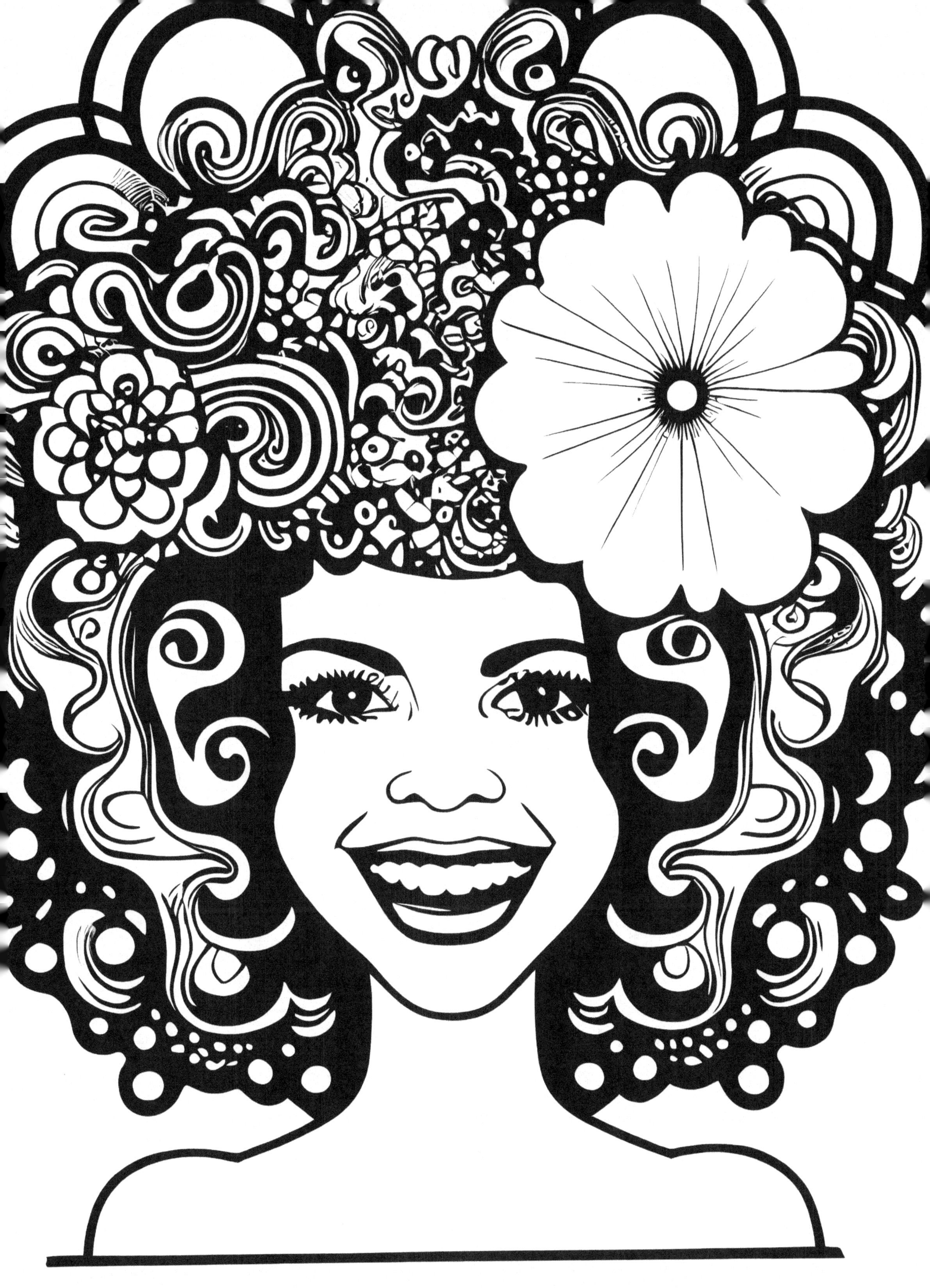

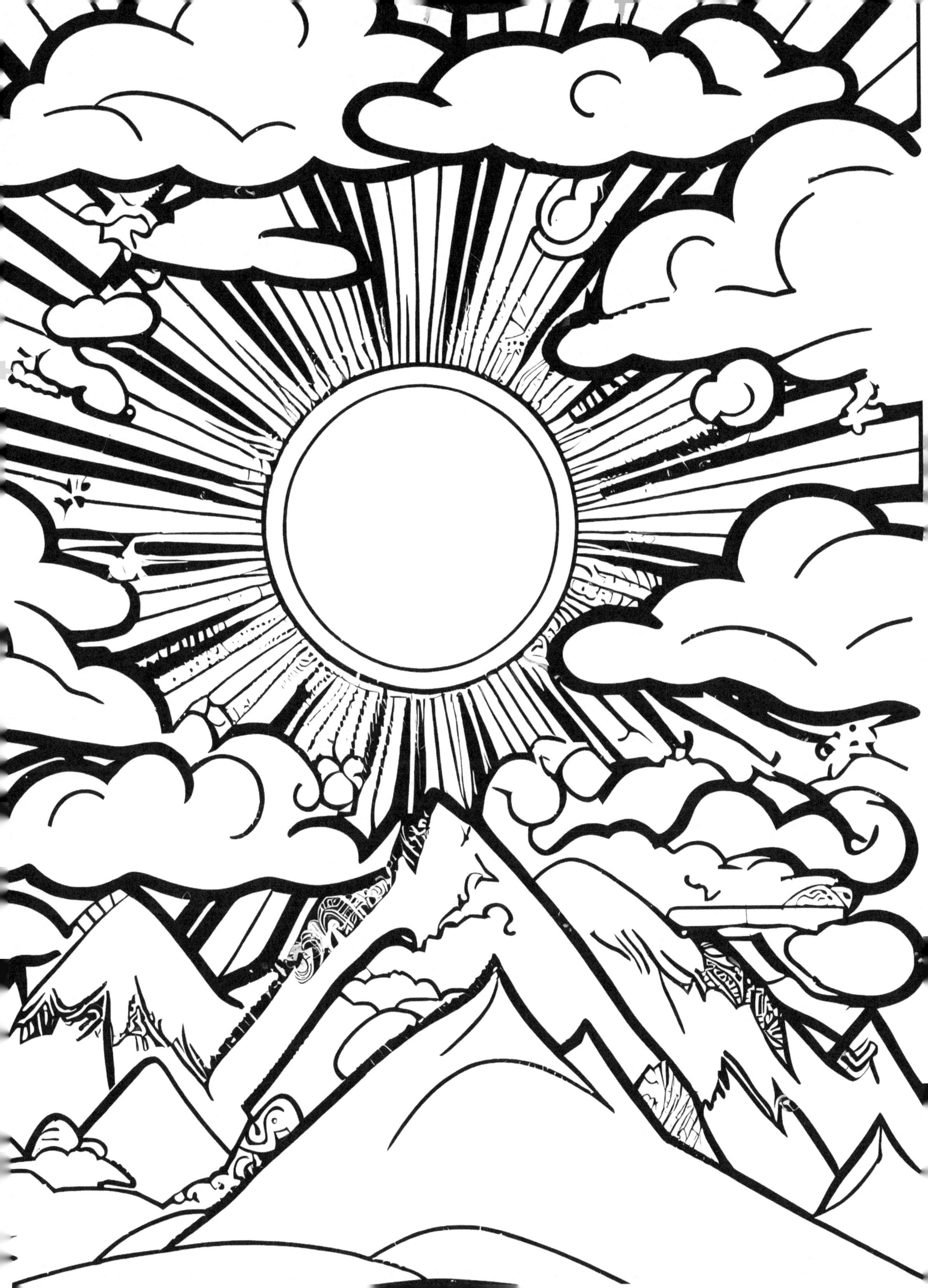

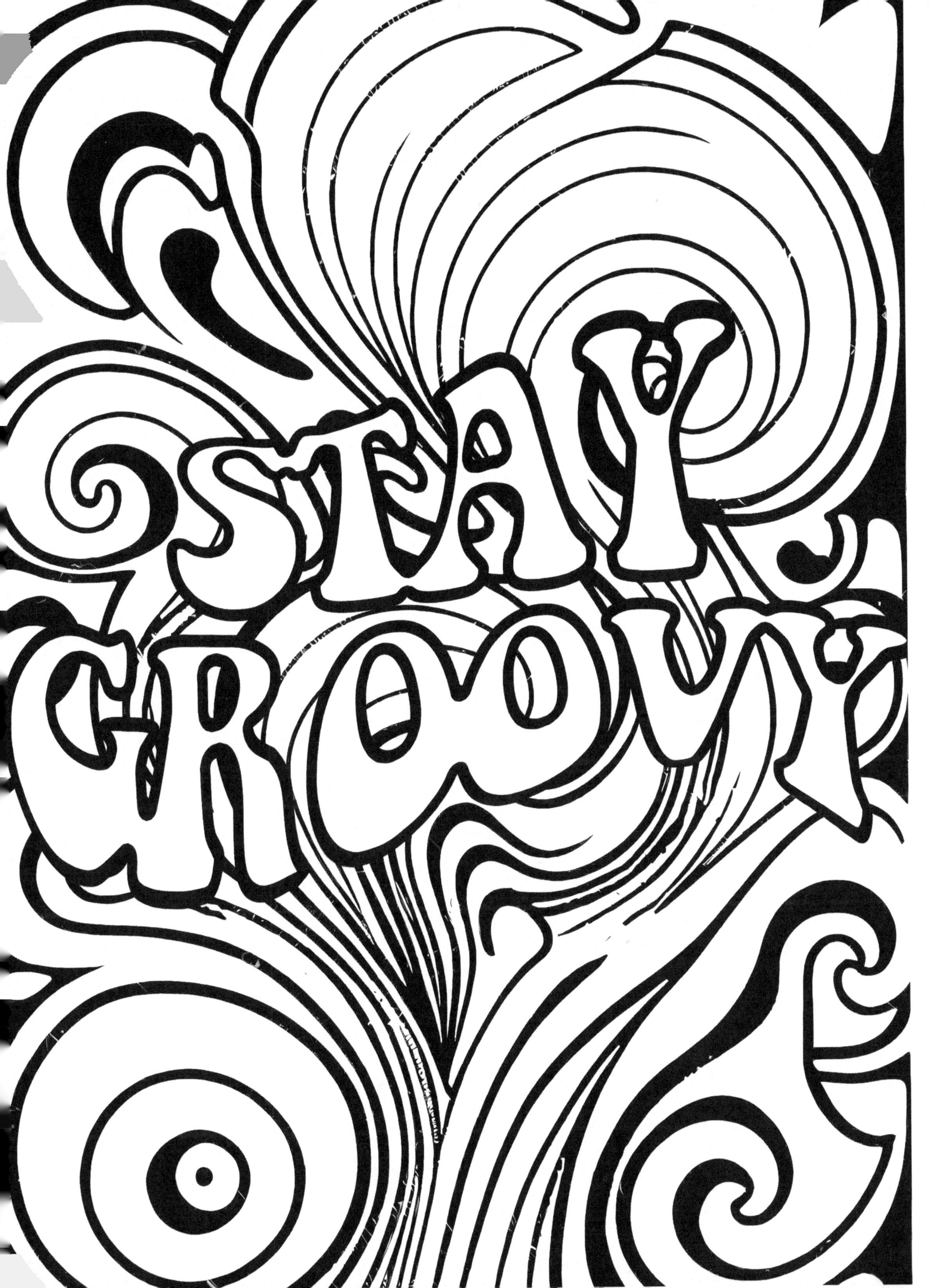
STAY
GROOVY

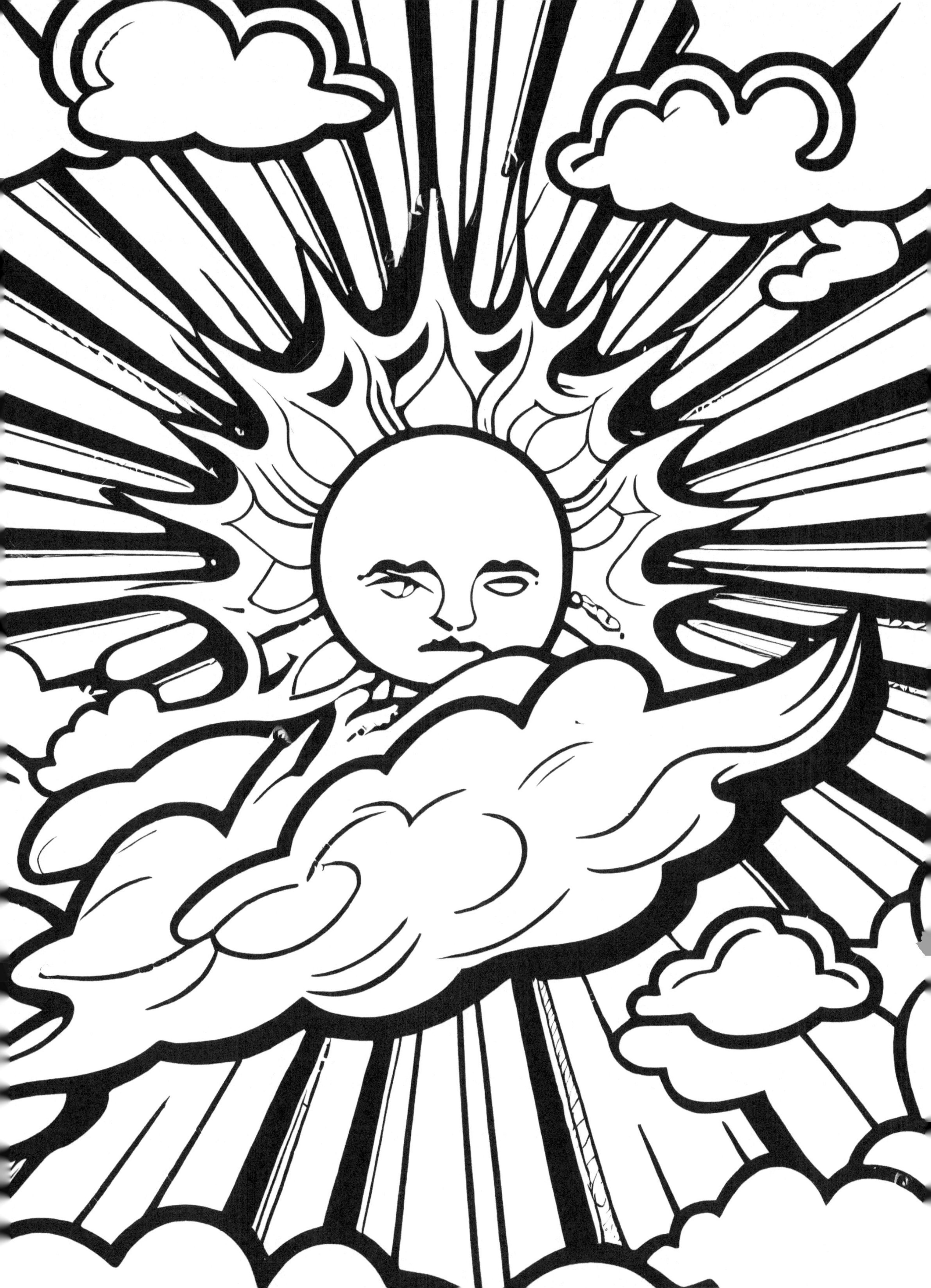

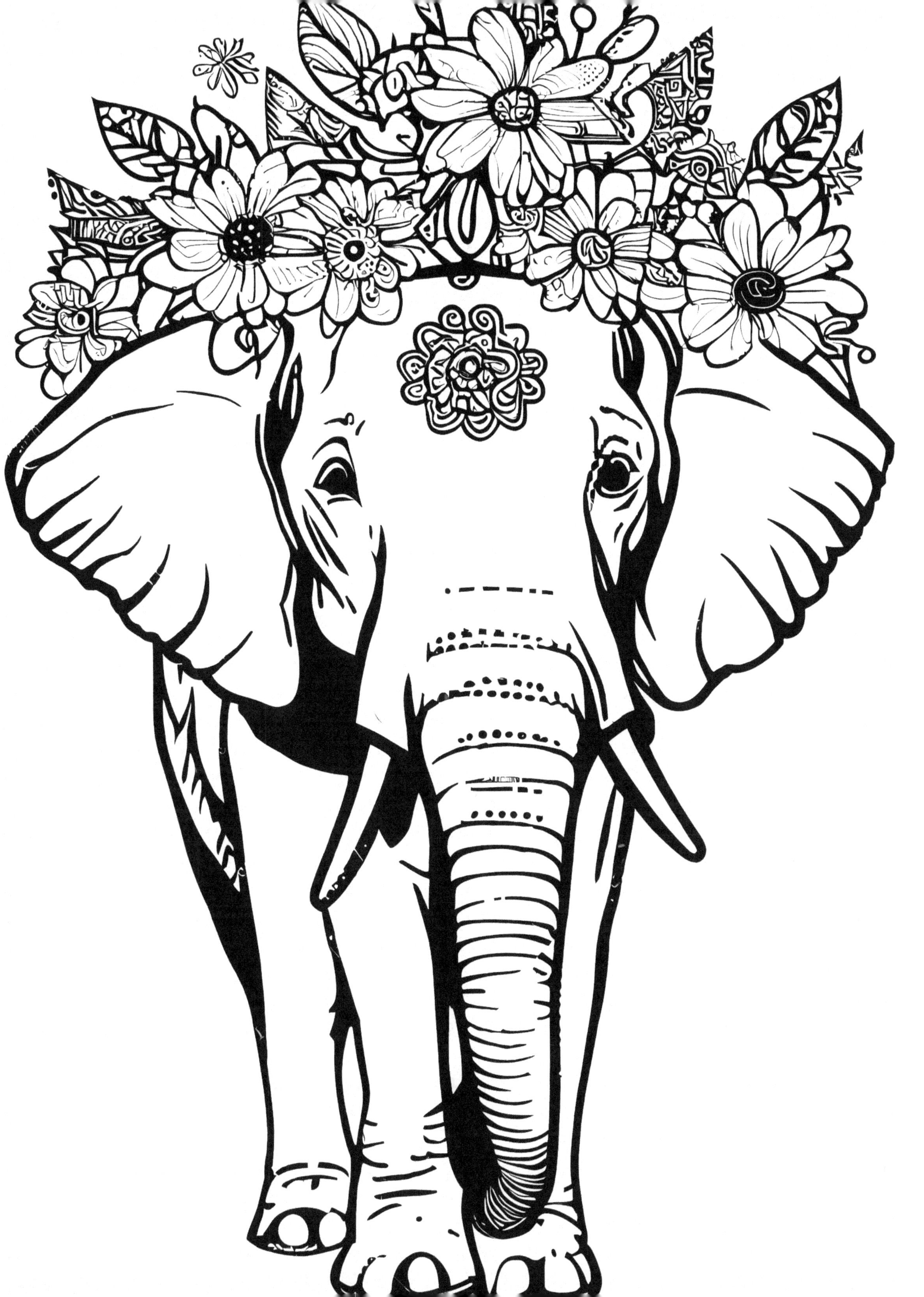

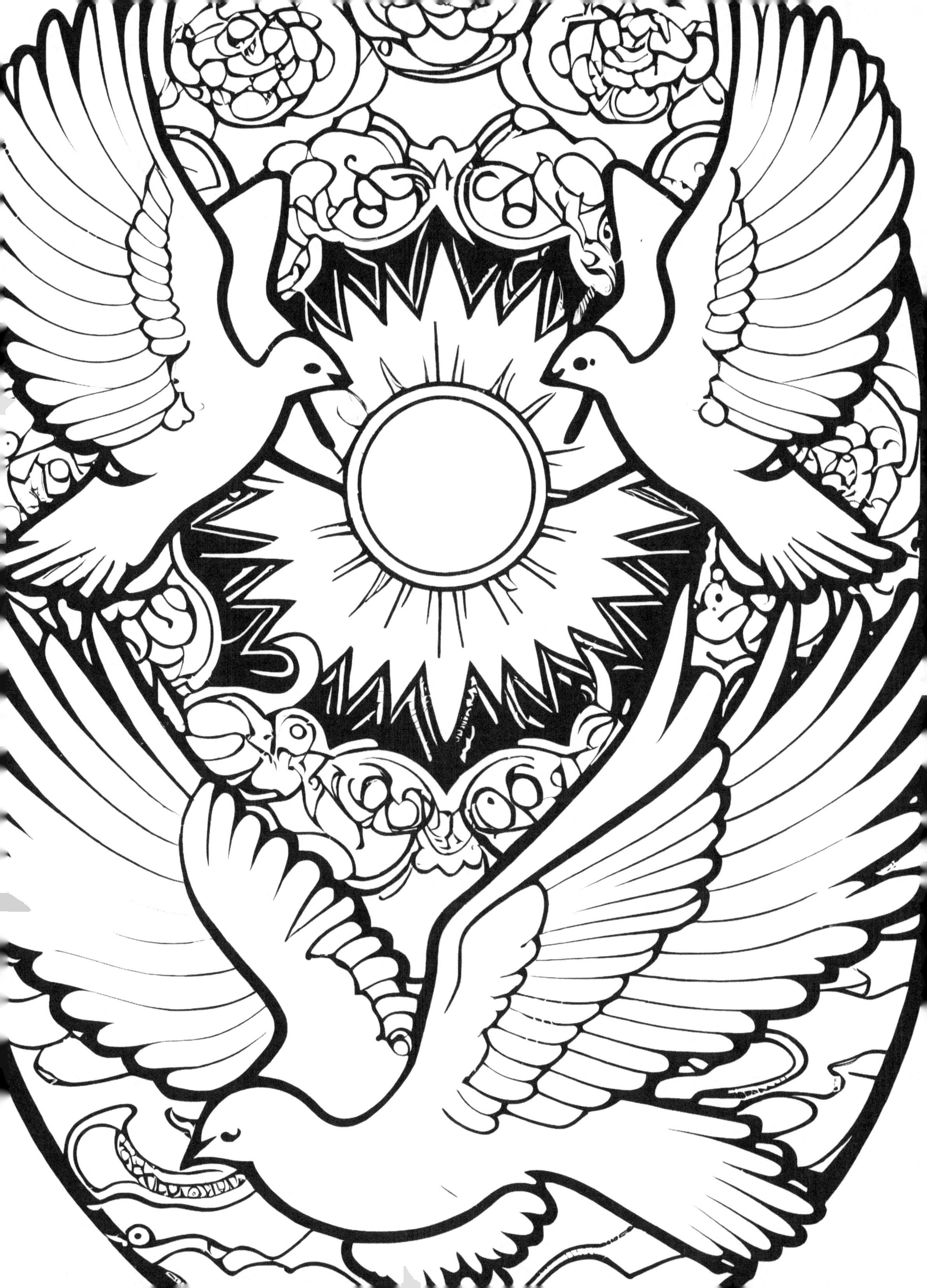

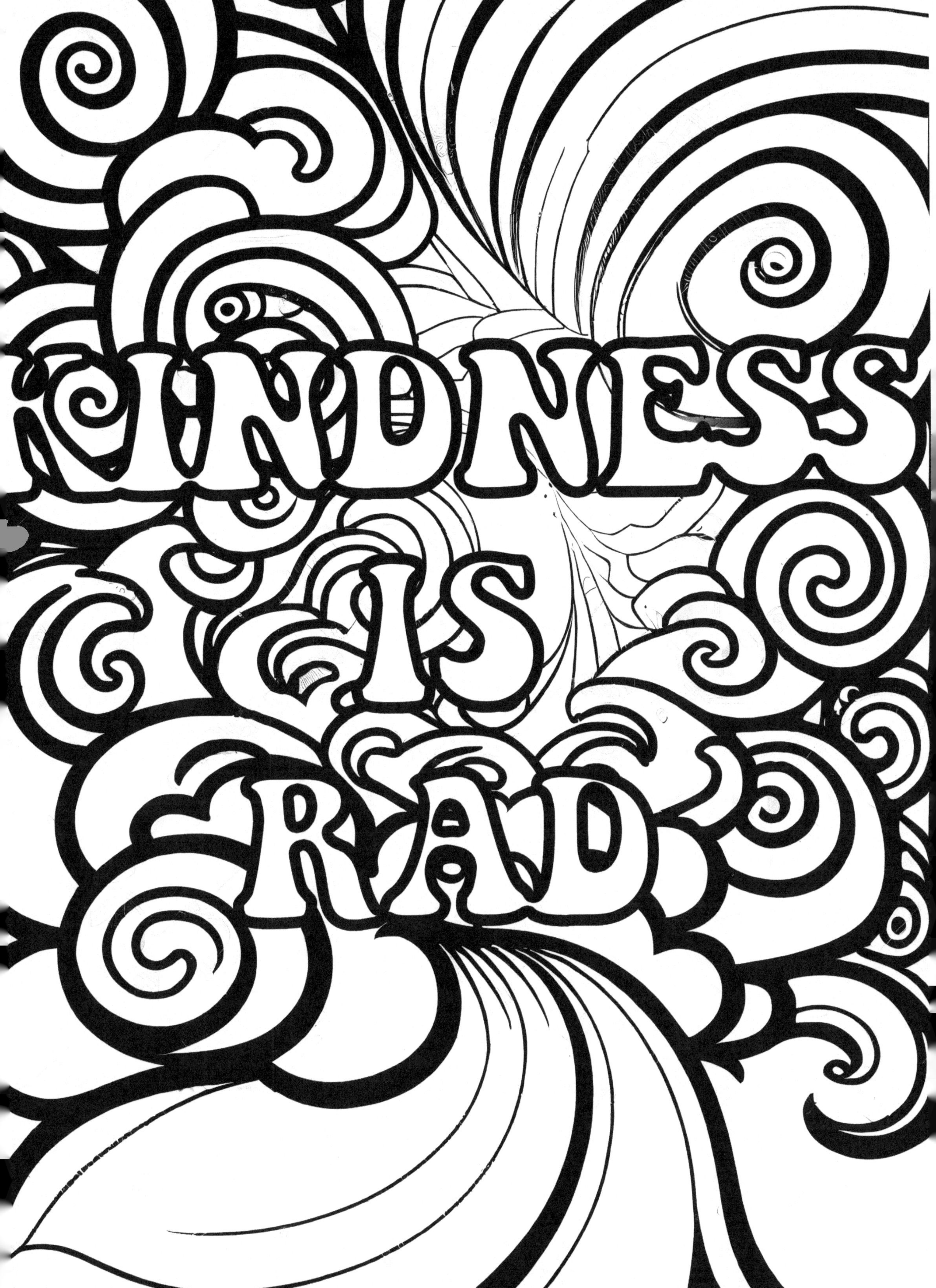
KINDNESS
IS
RAD

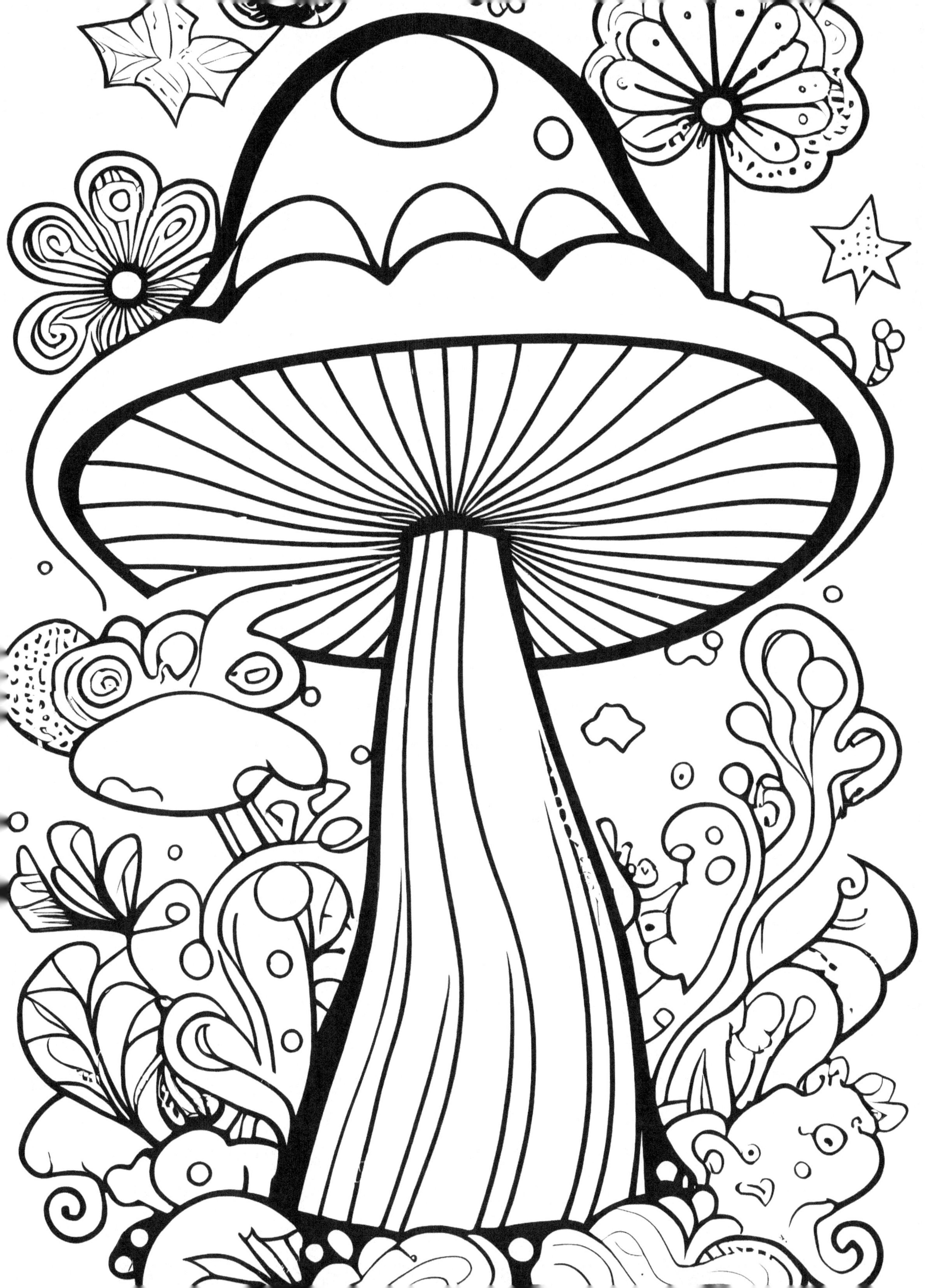

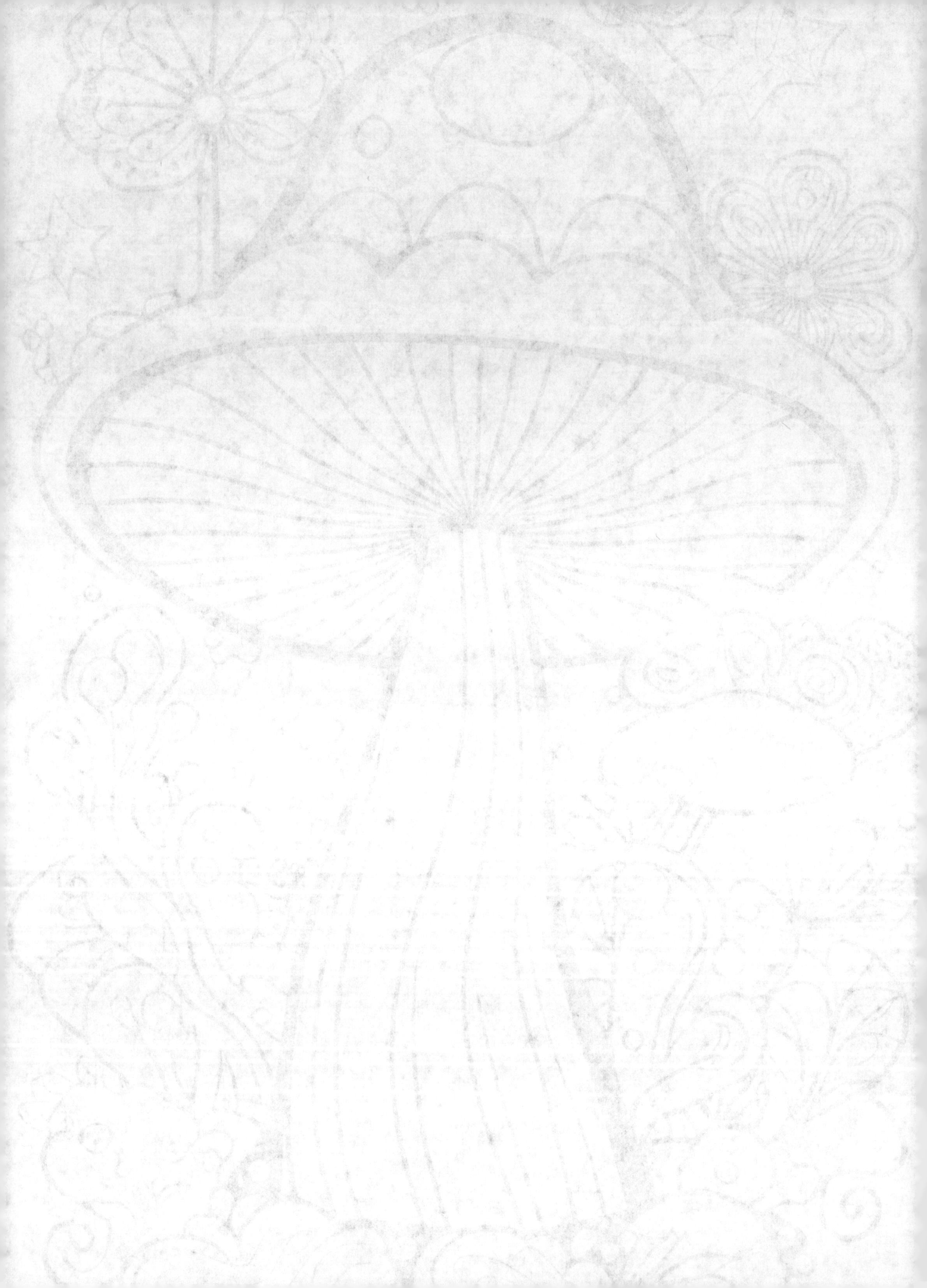

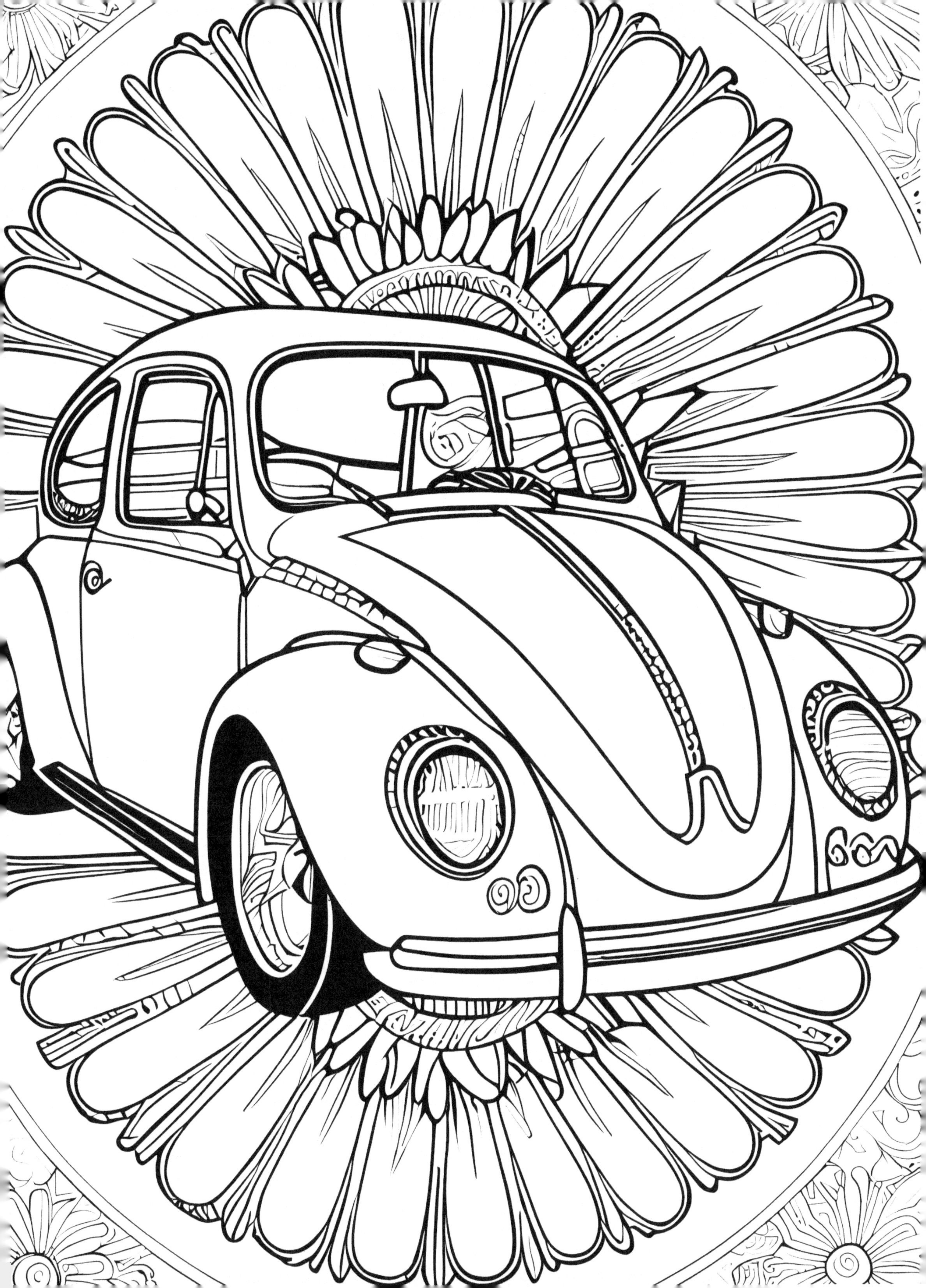

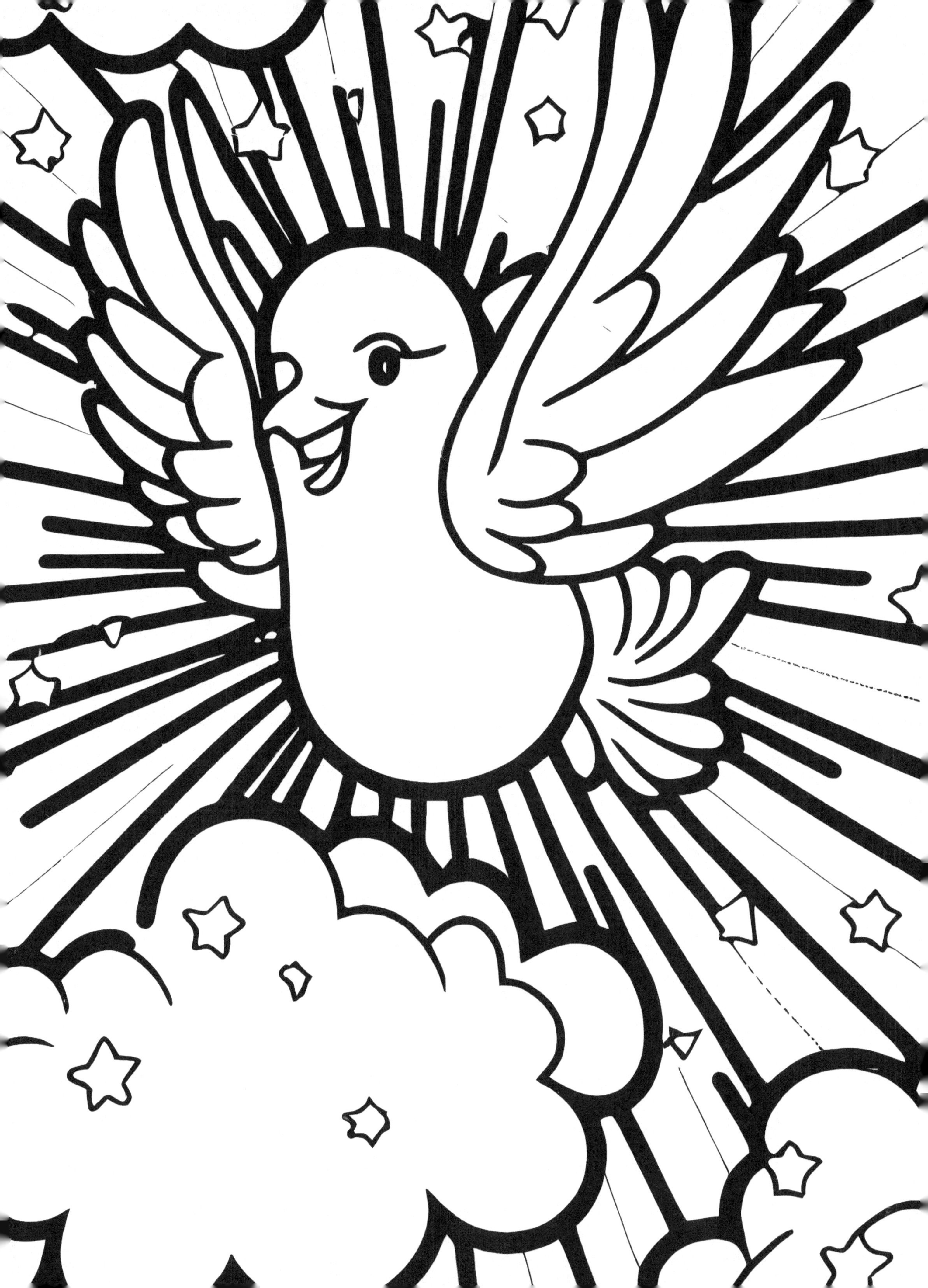

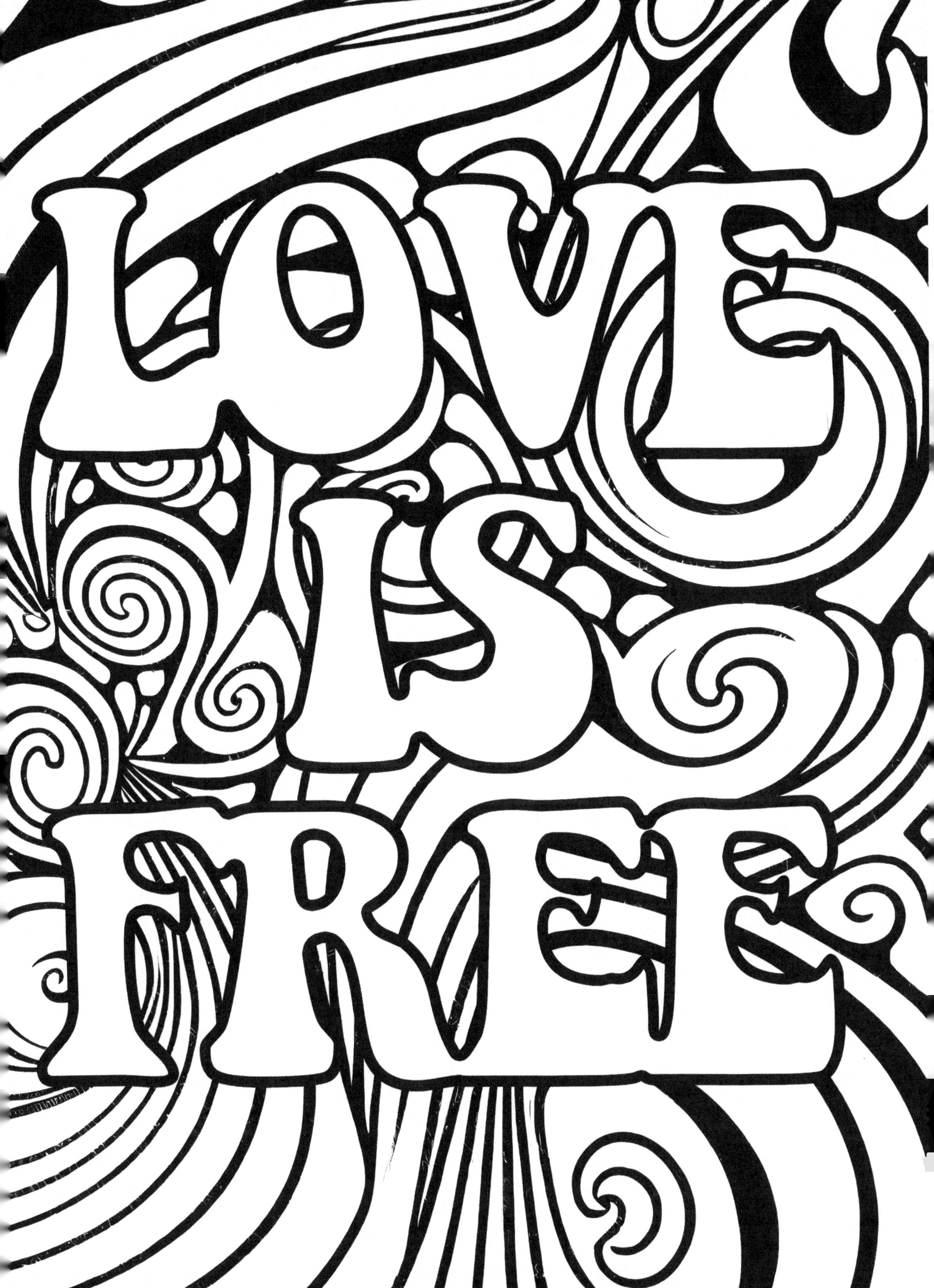

LOVE
IS
FREE

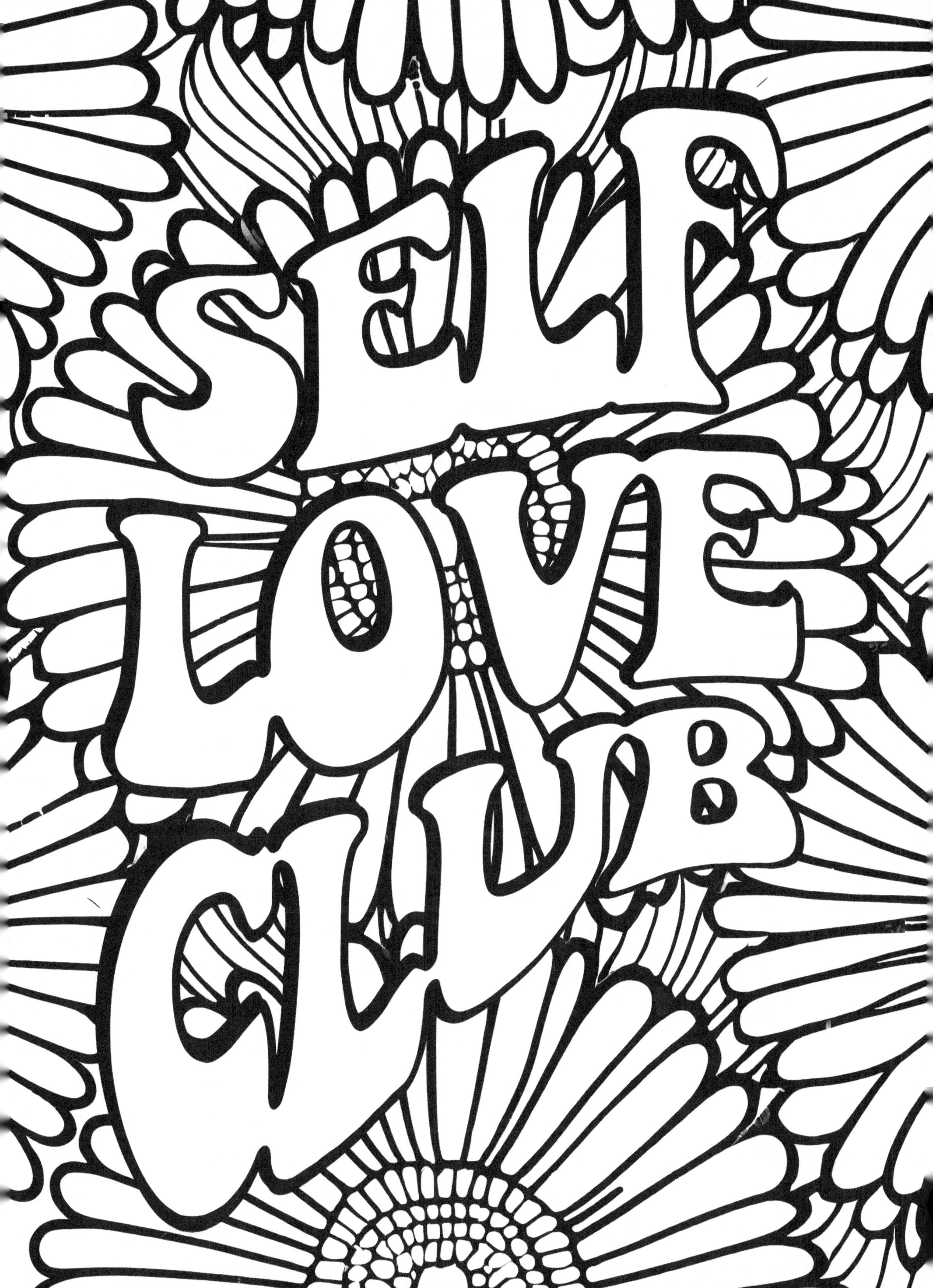
SELF
LOVE
CLUB

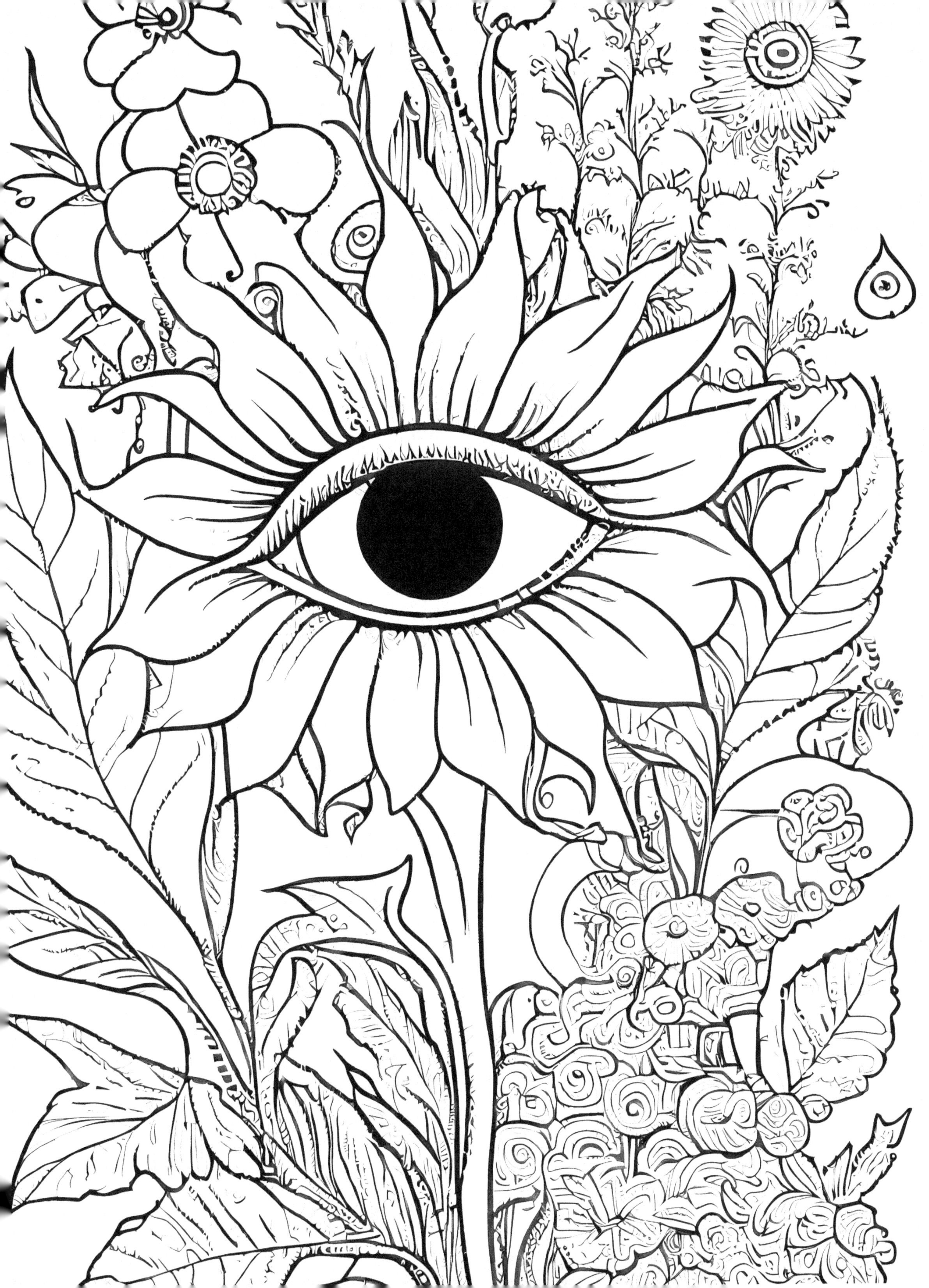

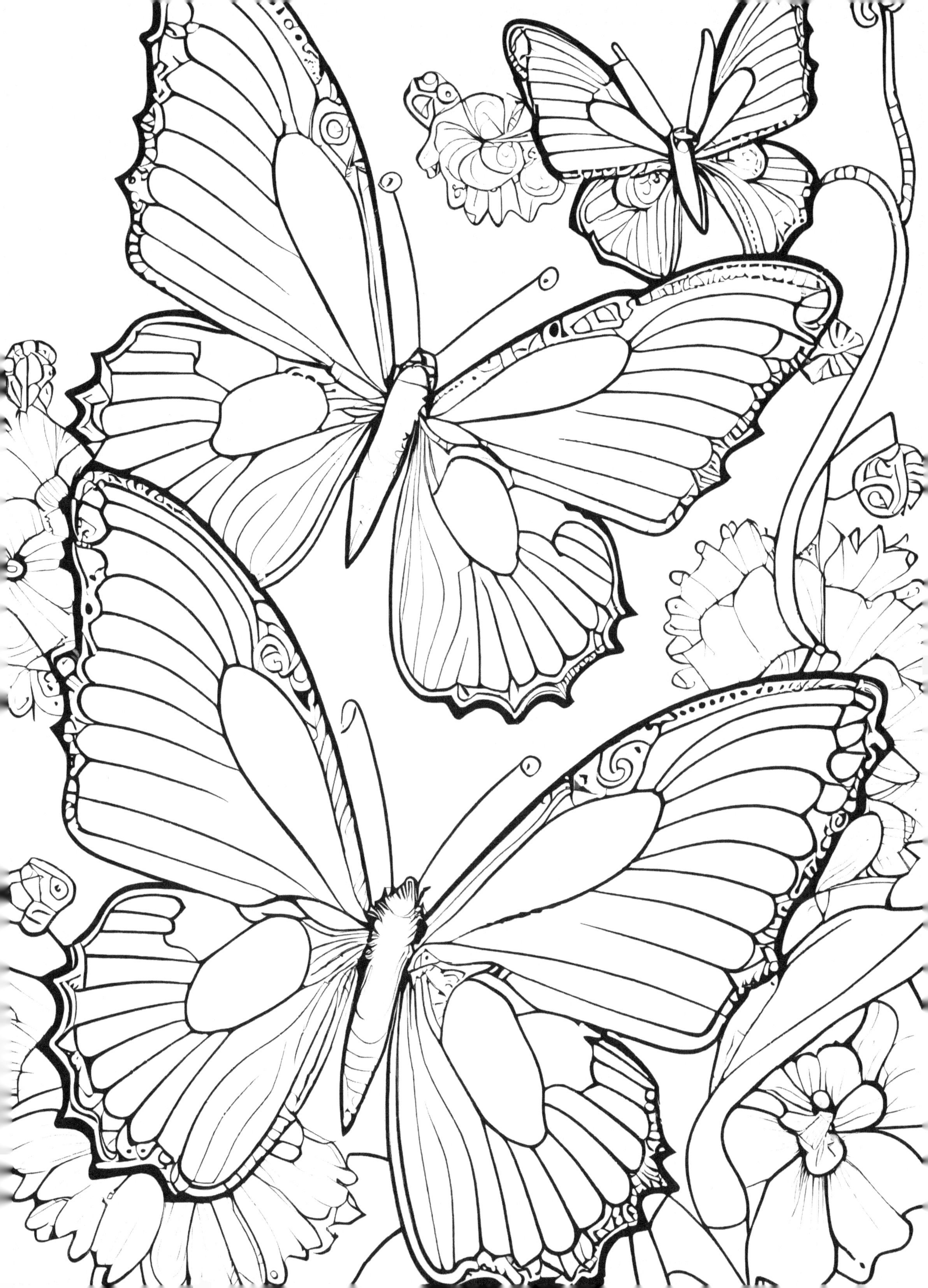

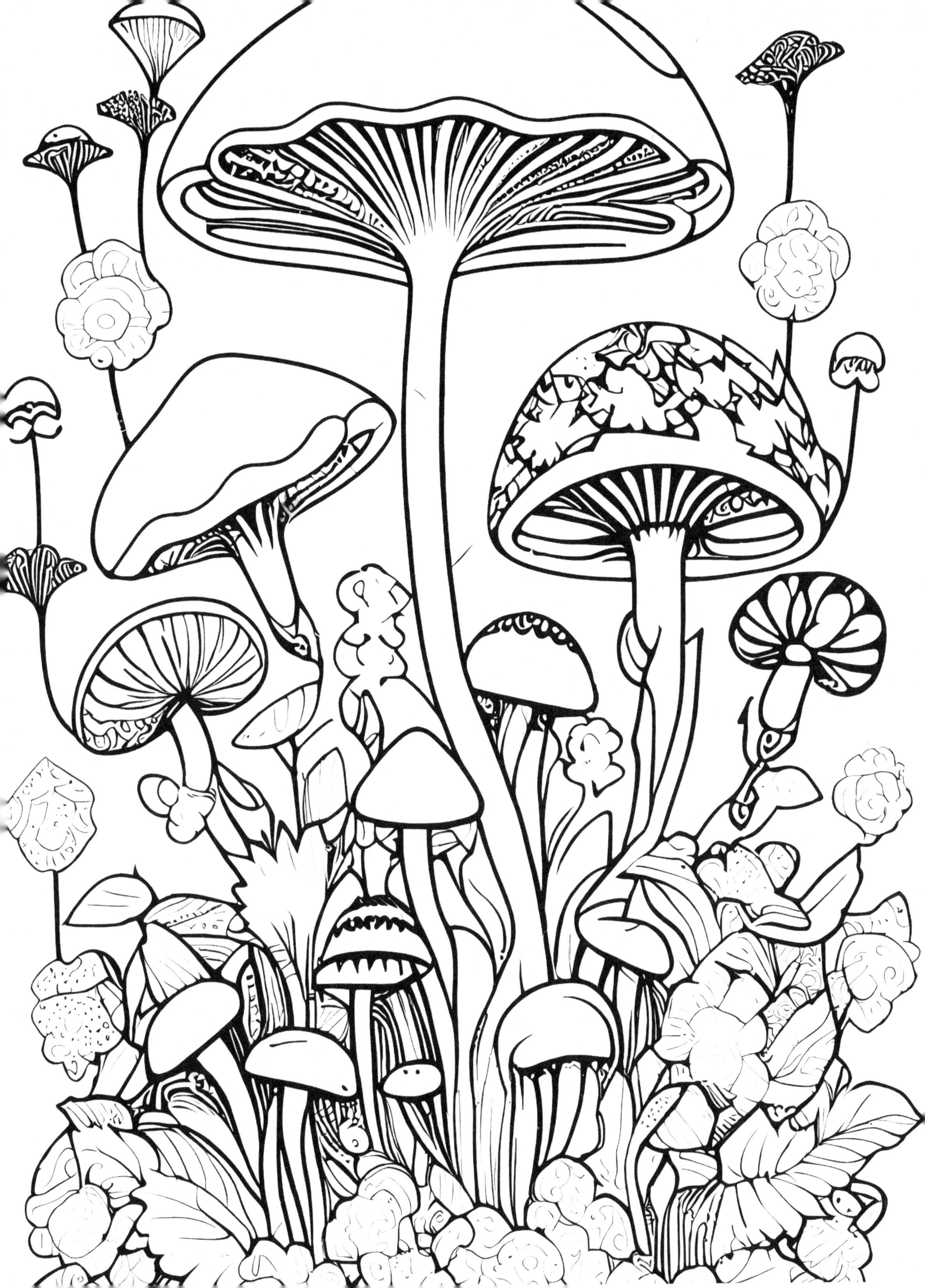

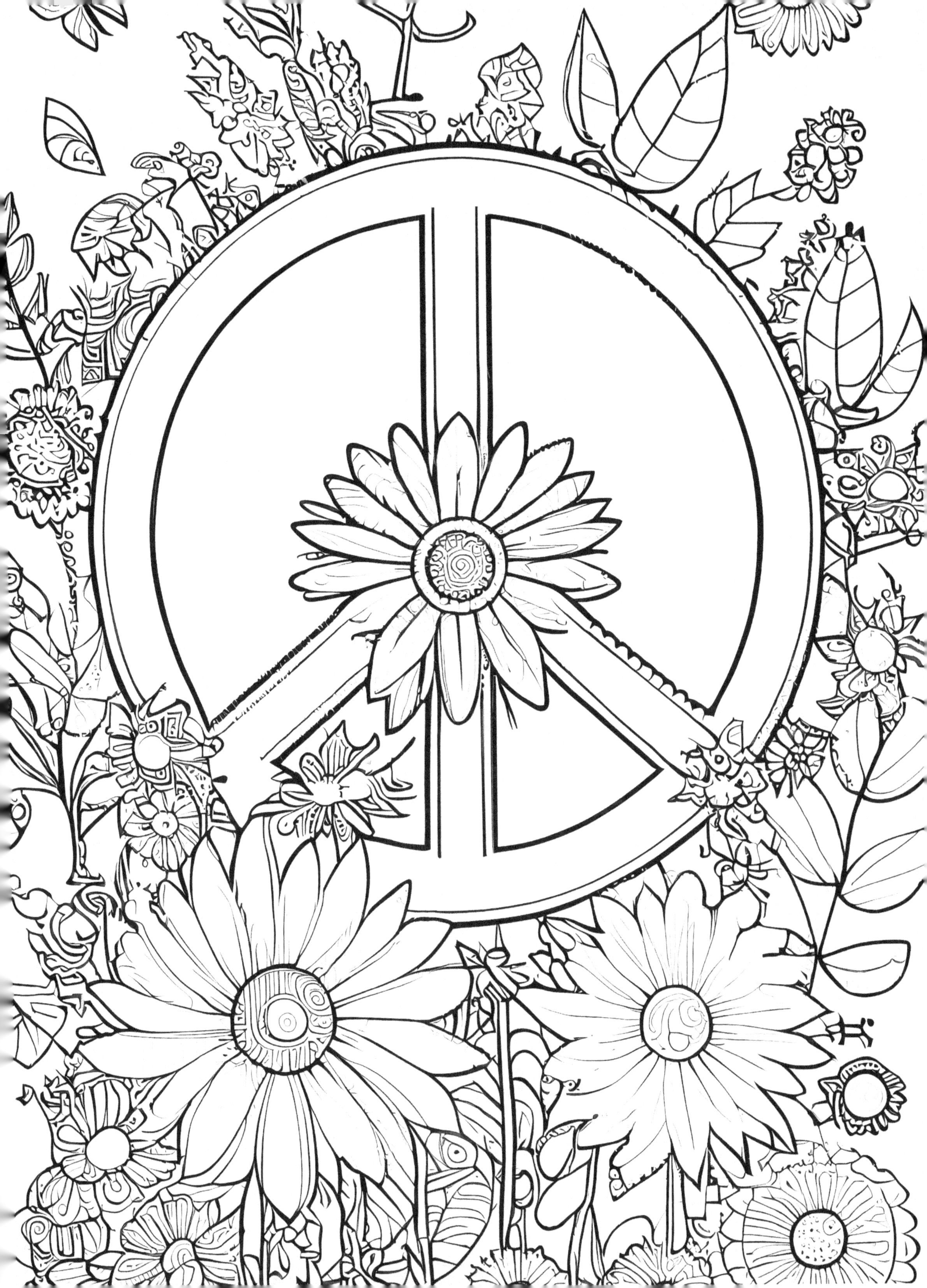

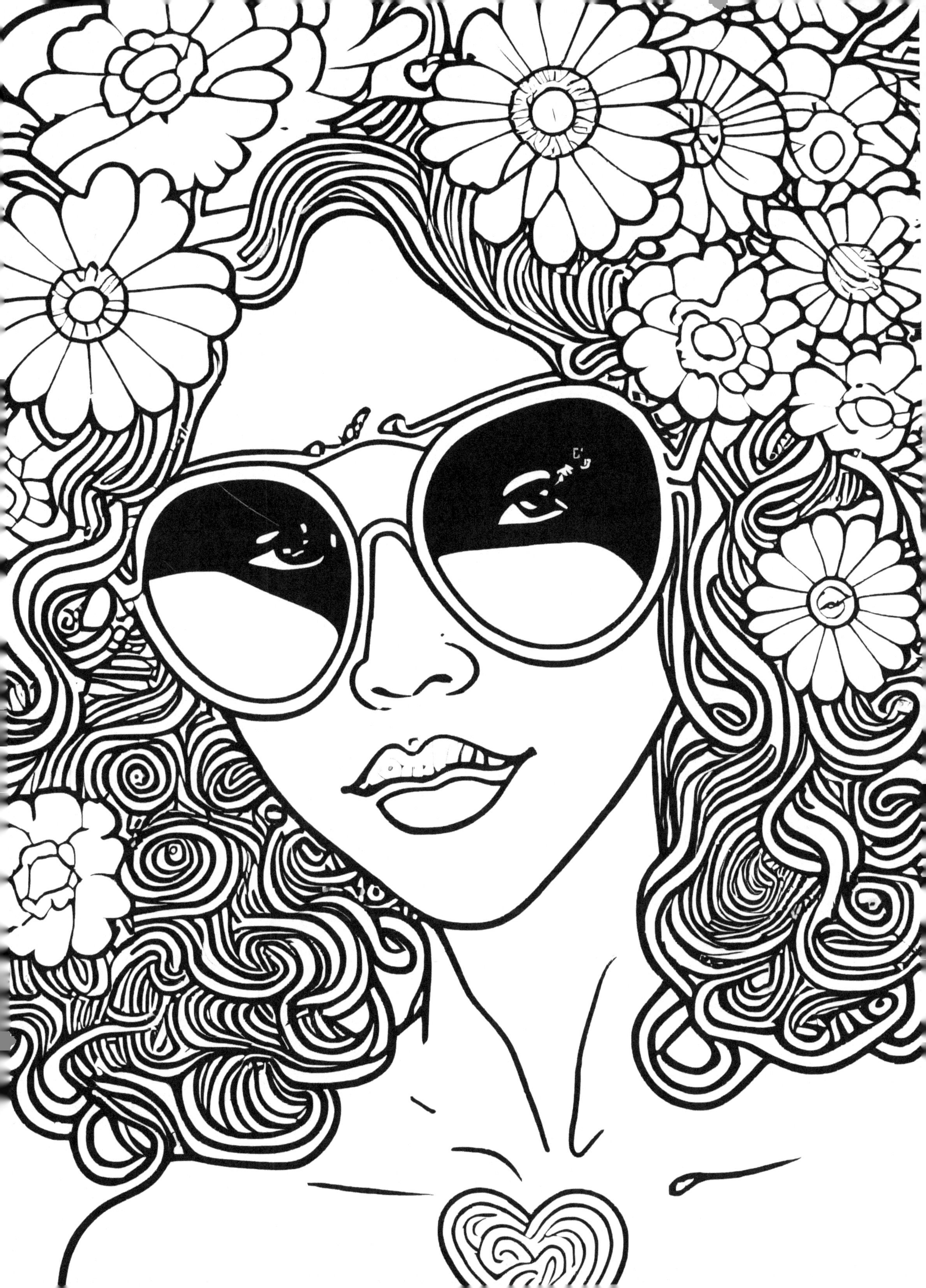

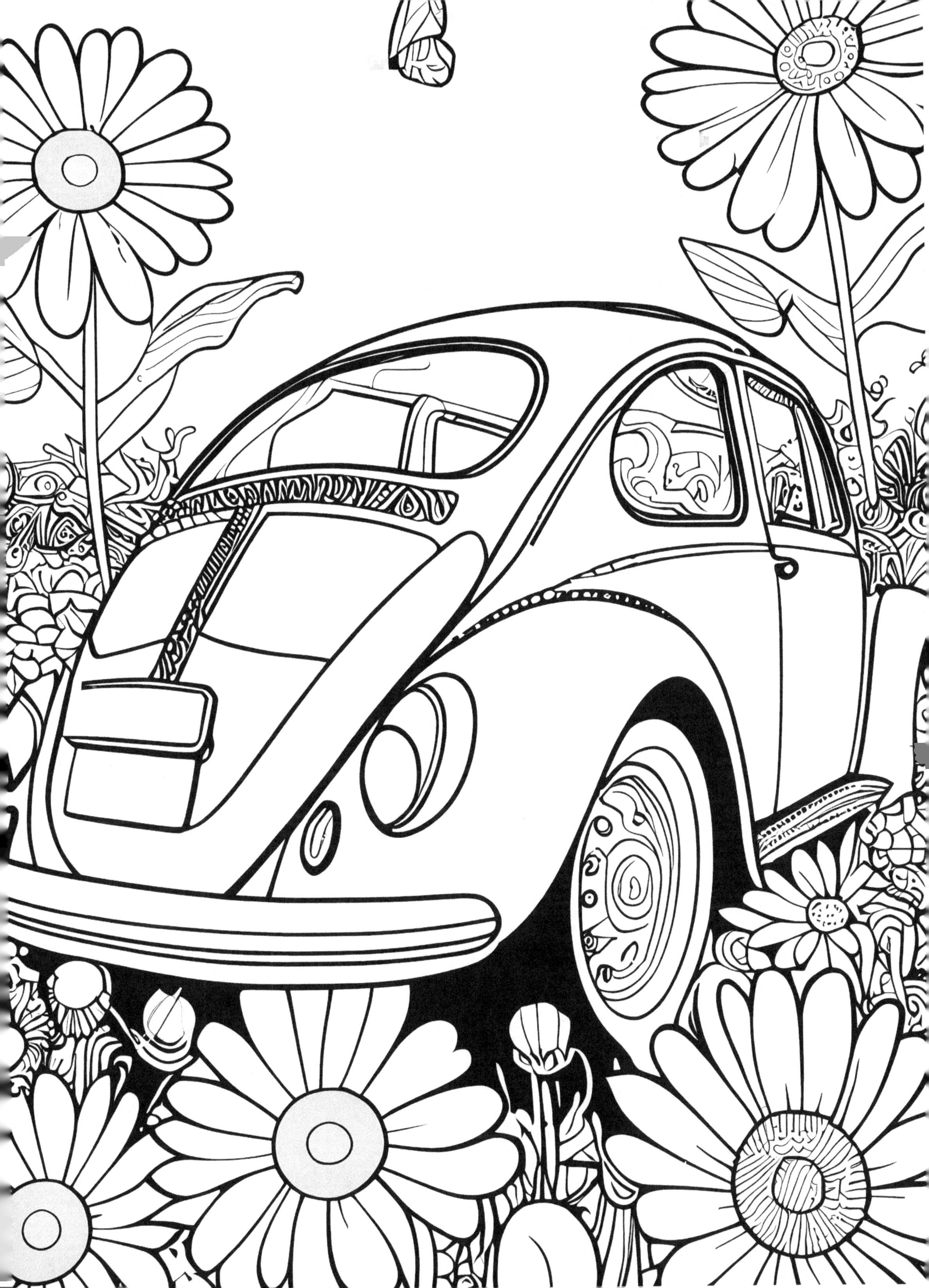

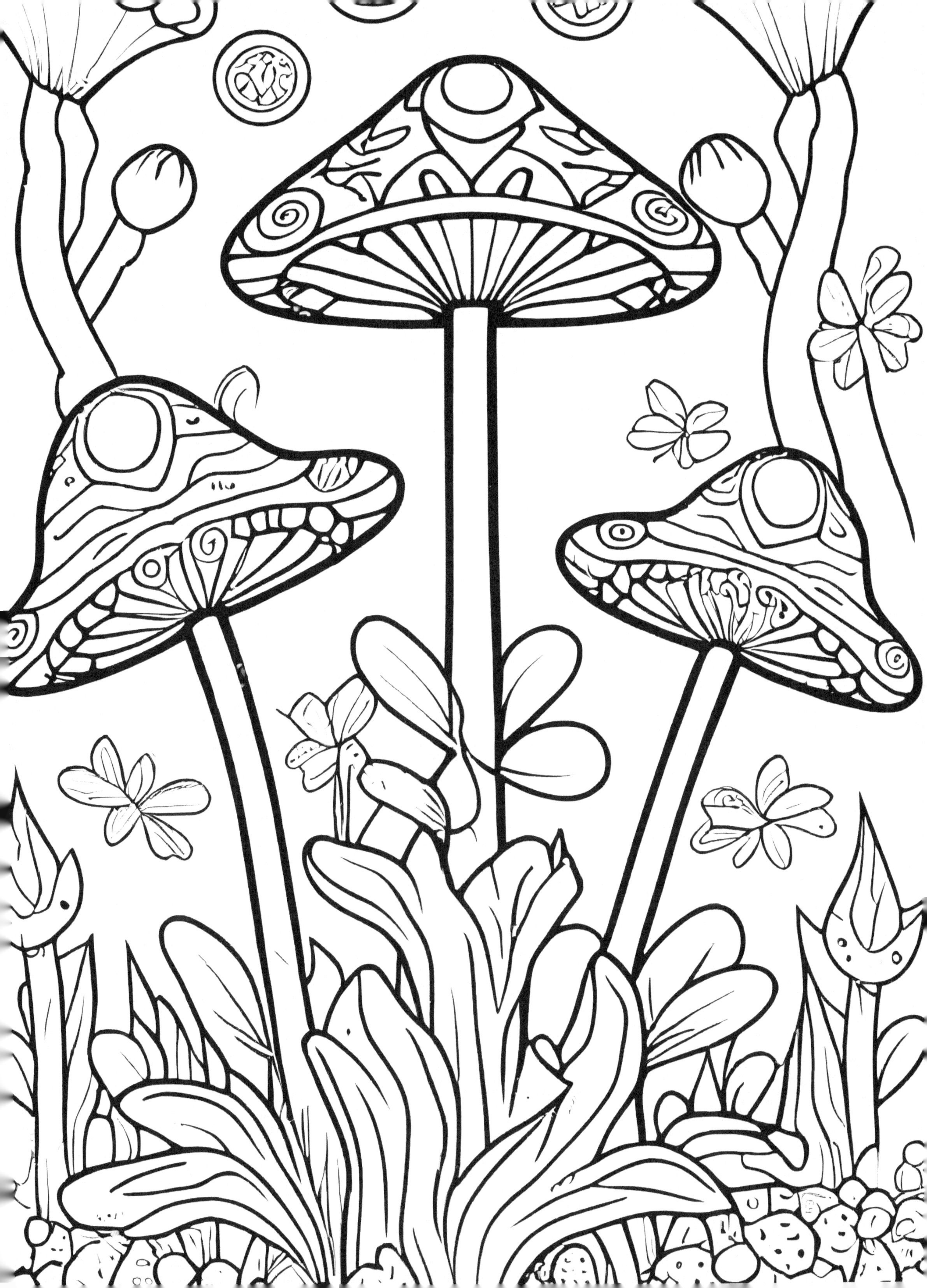

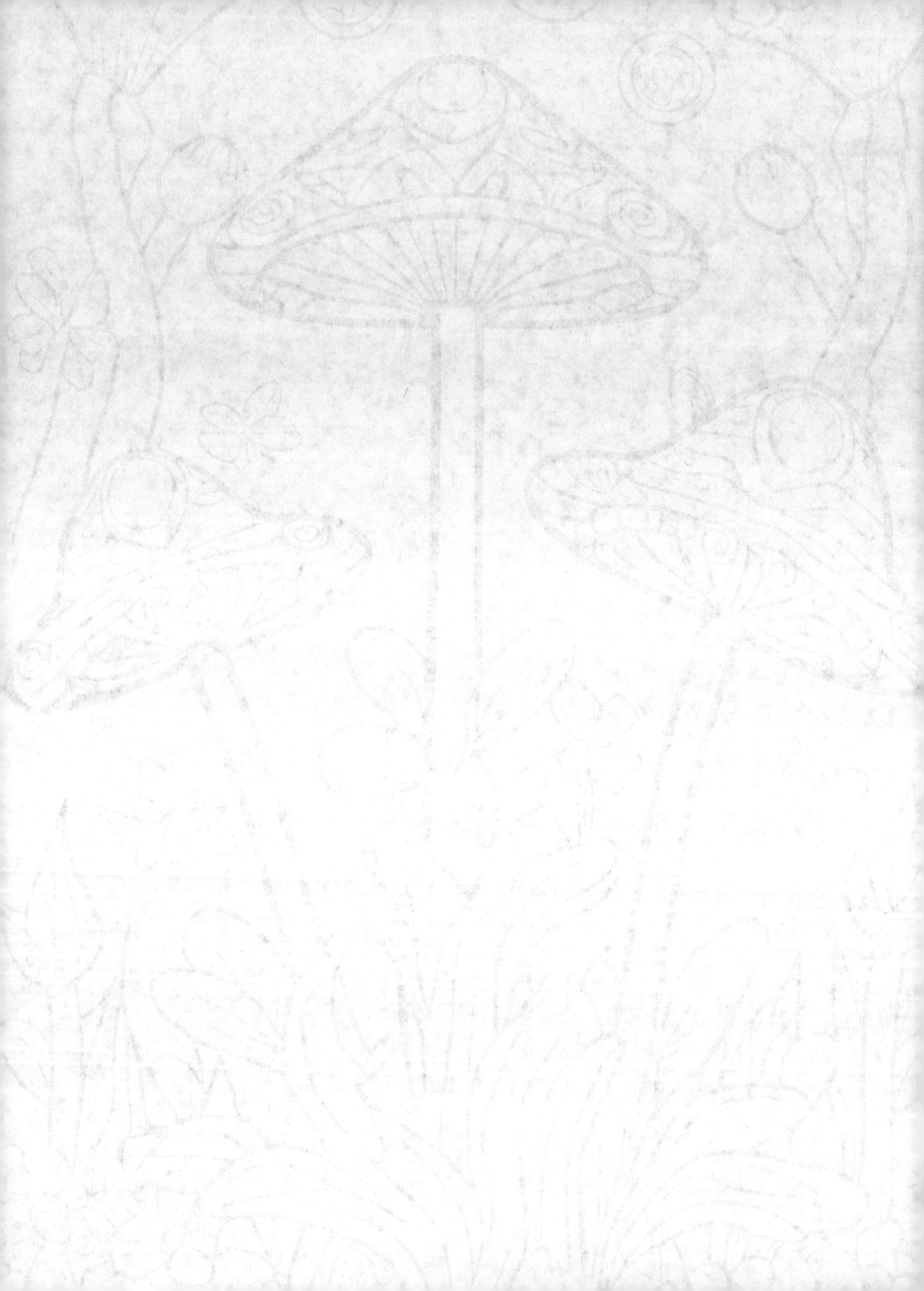

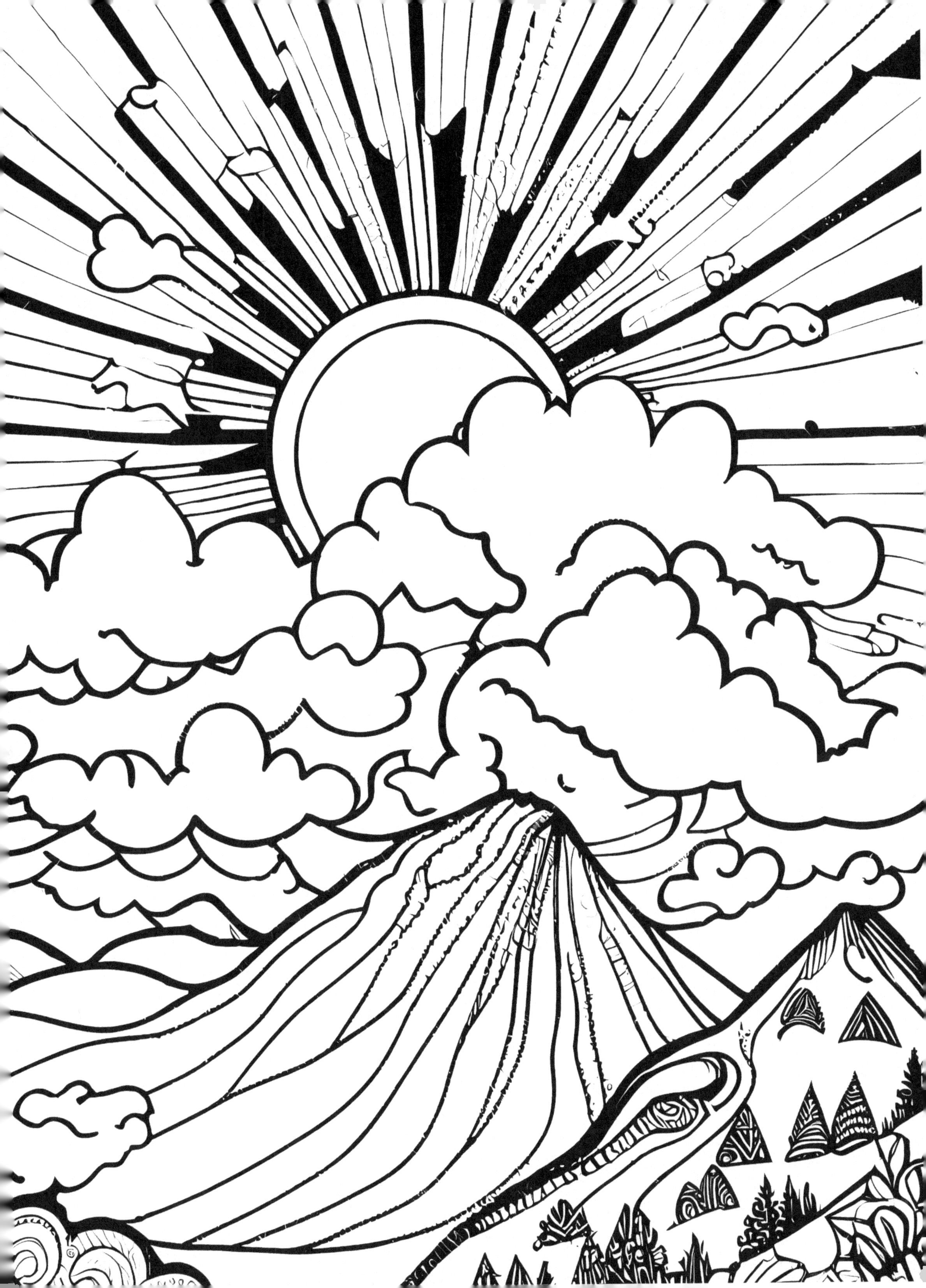

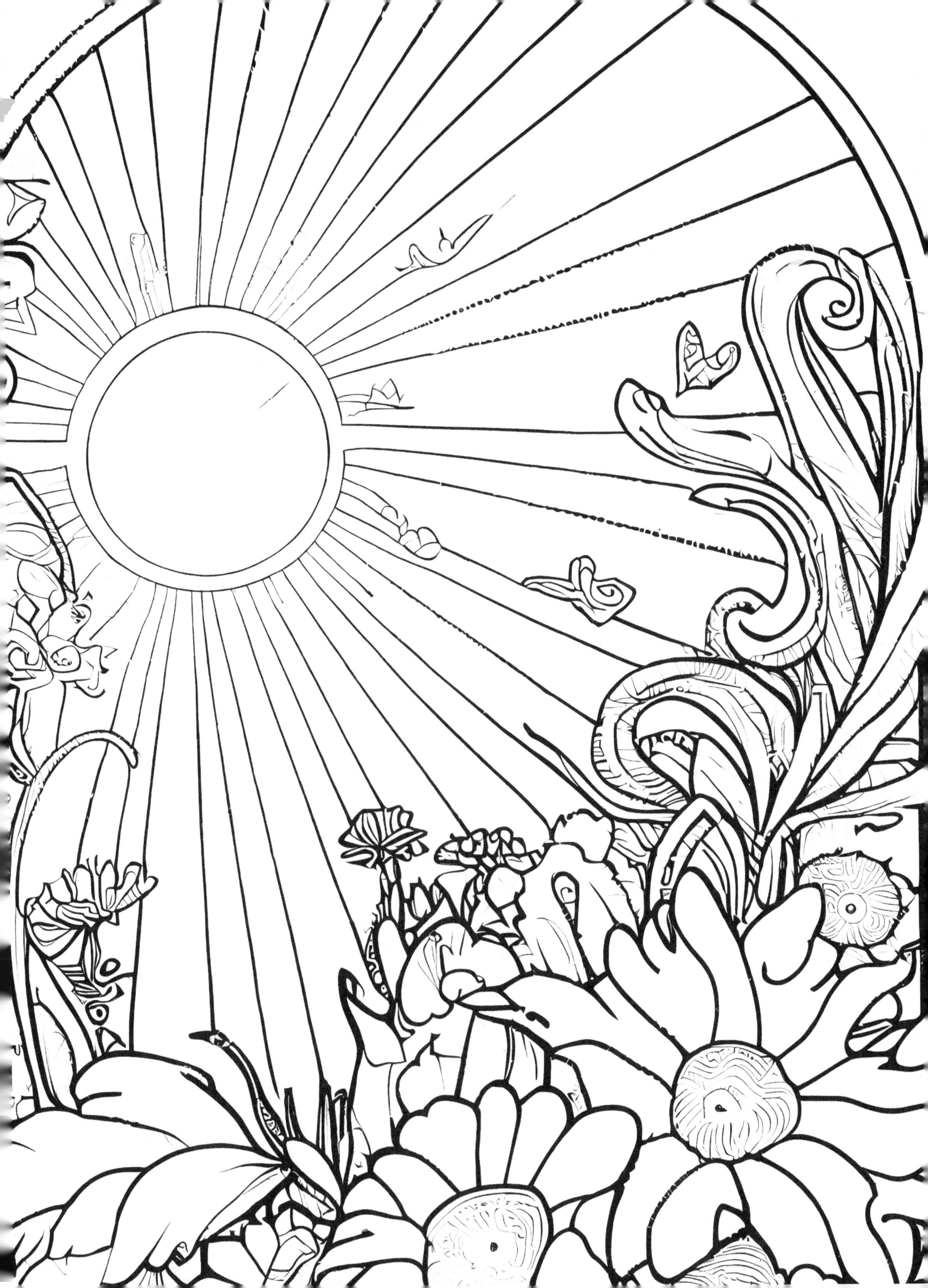

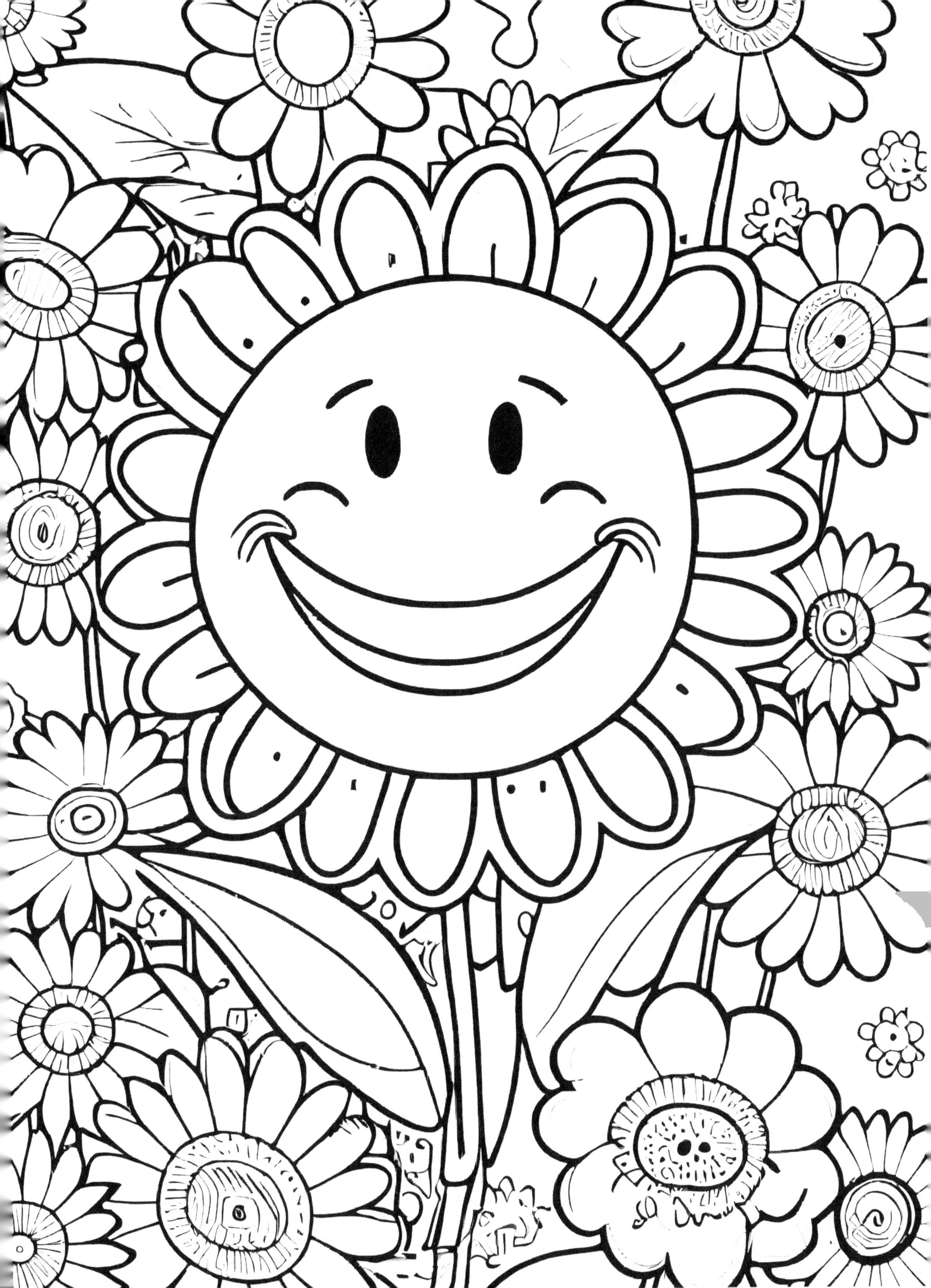

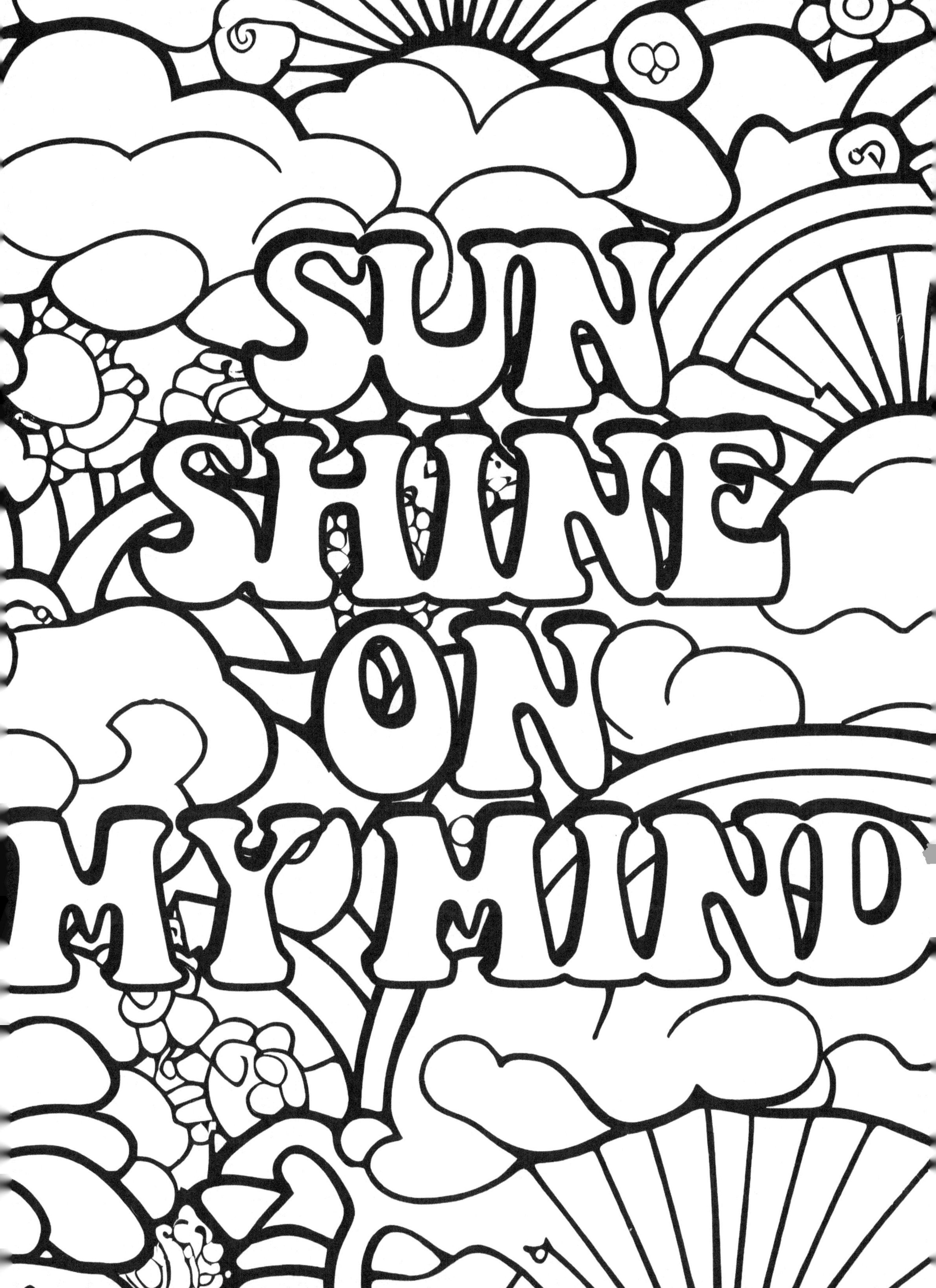

SUN
SHINE
ON
MY MIND

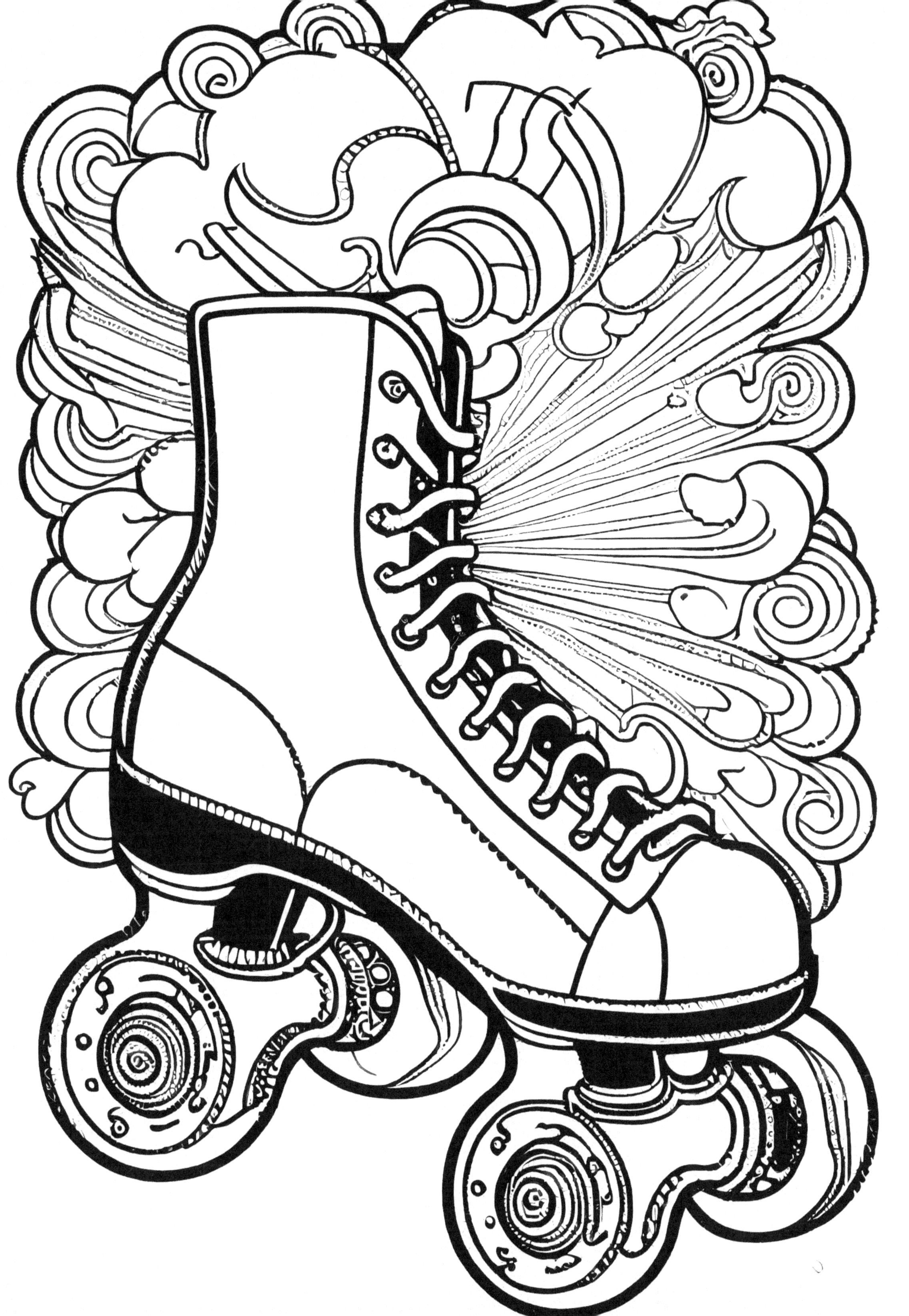

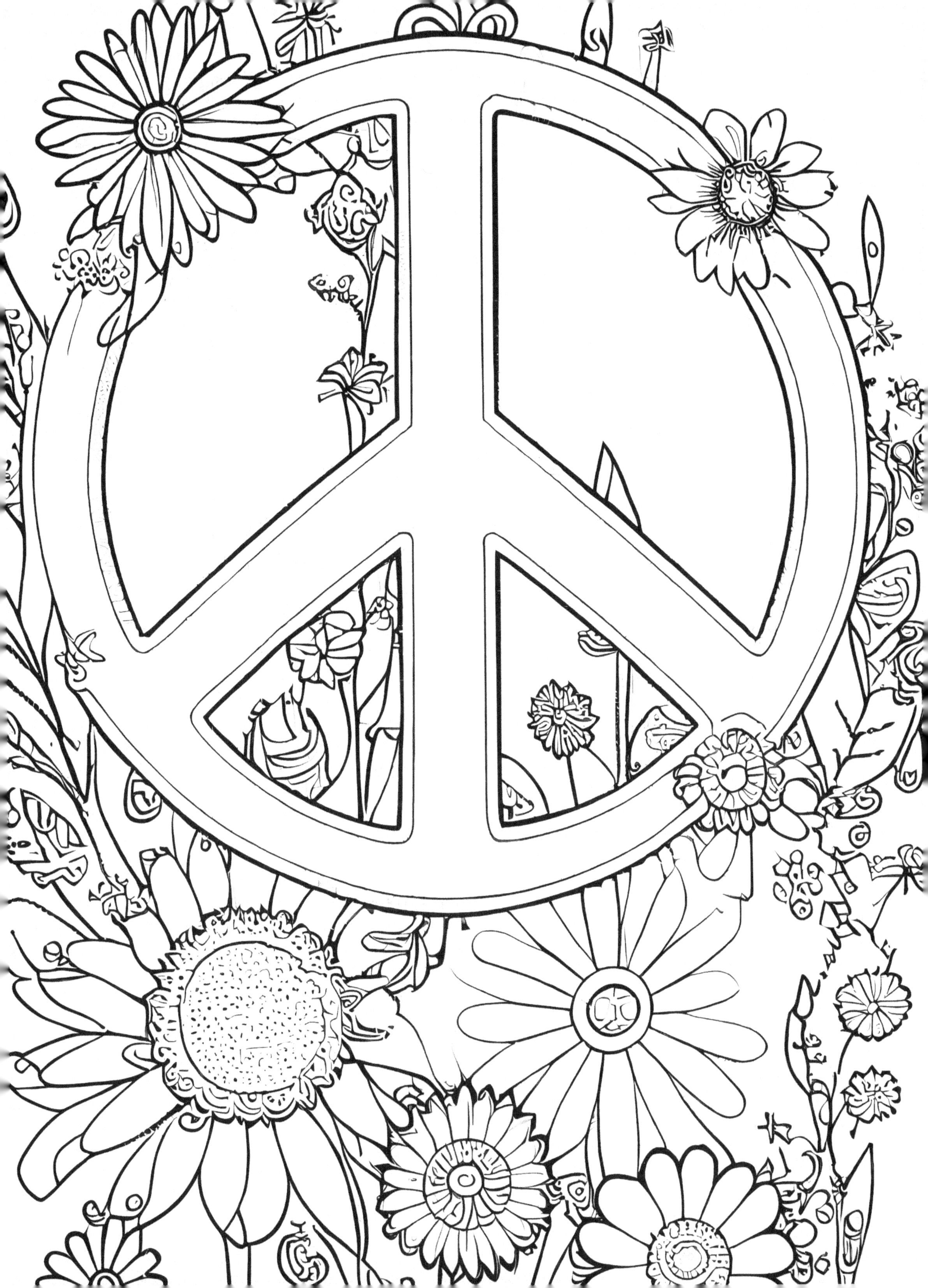

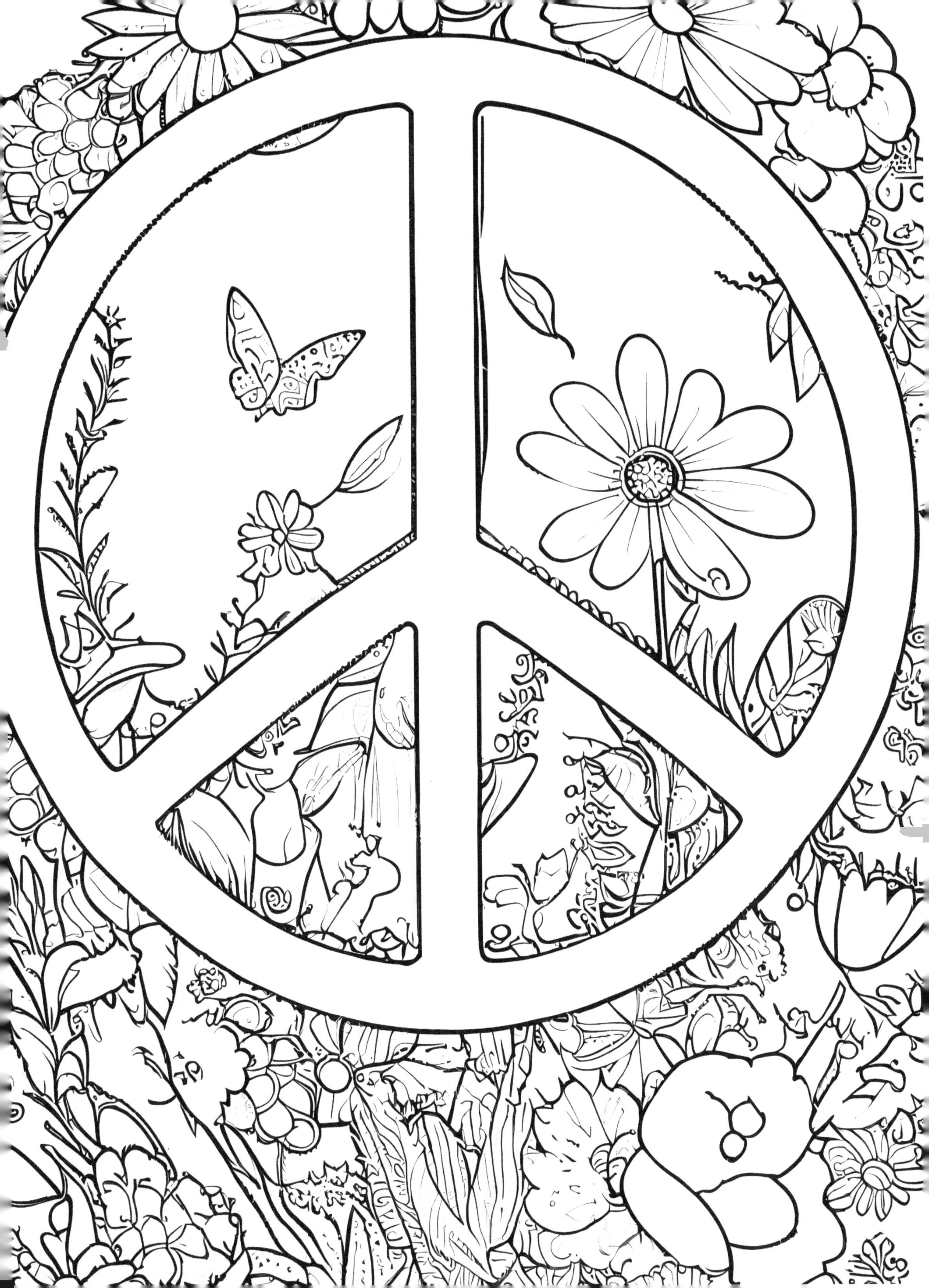

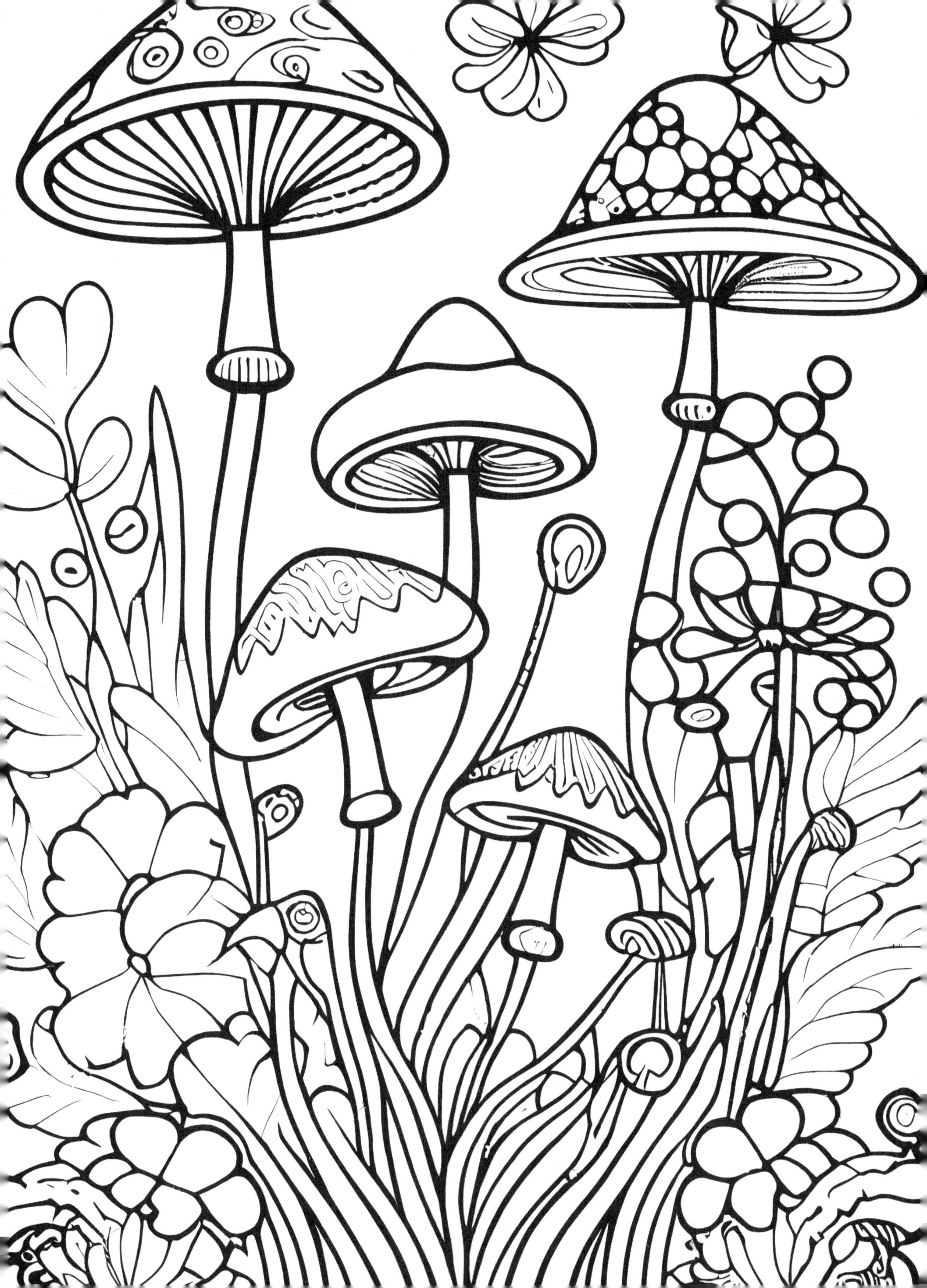

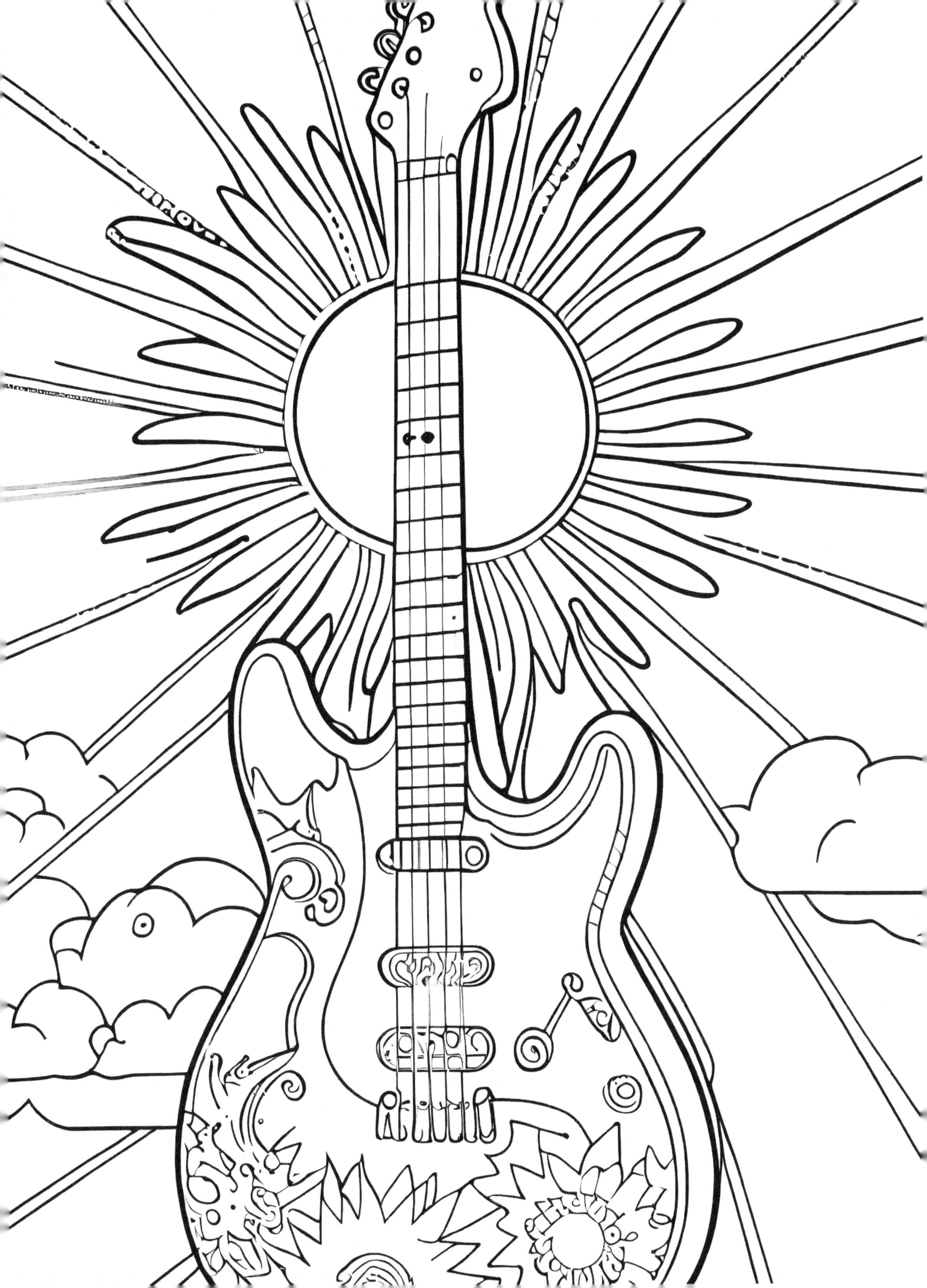

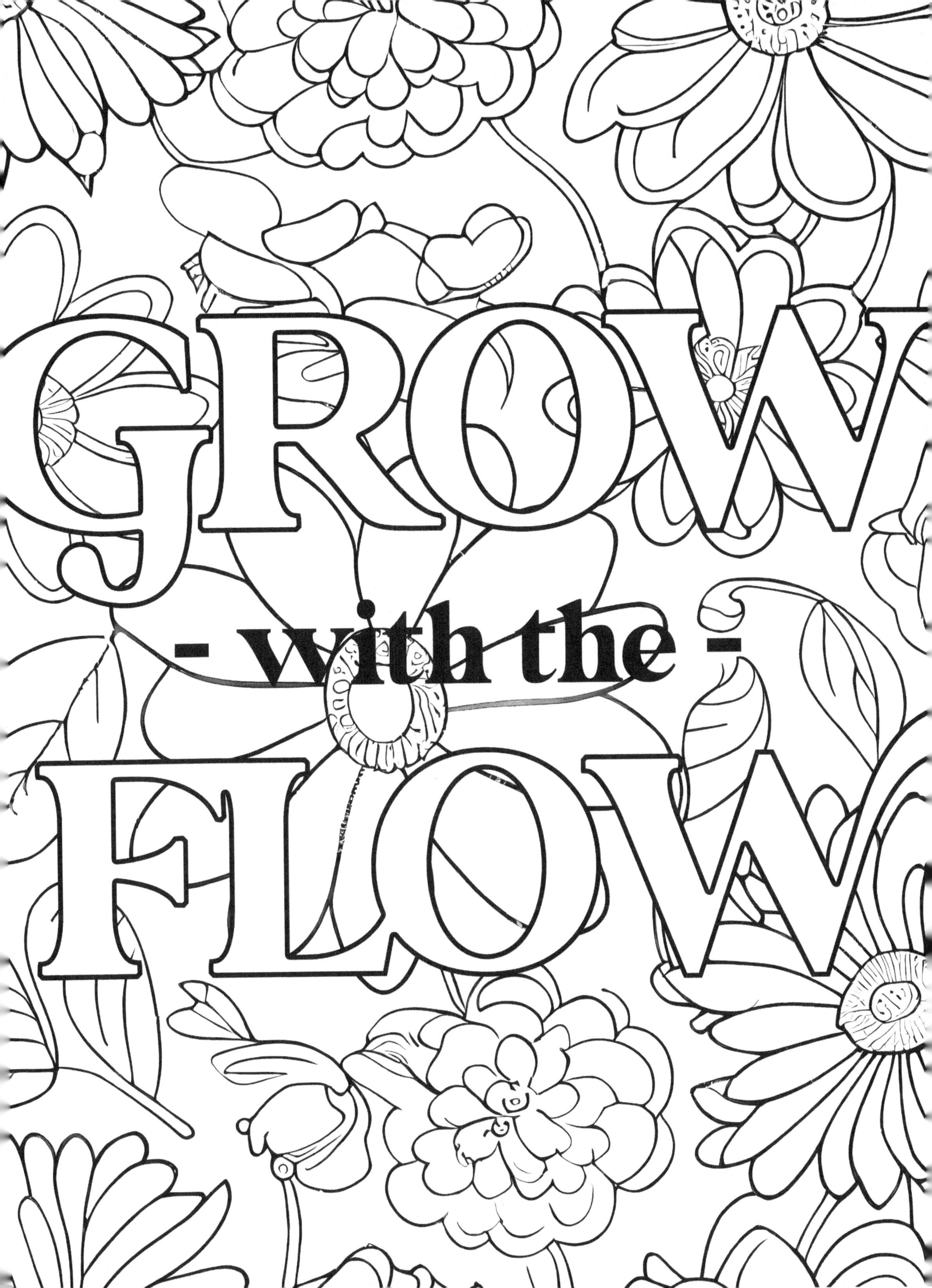
GROW
- with the -
FLOW

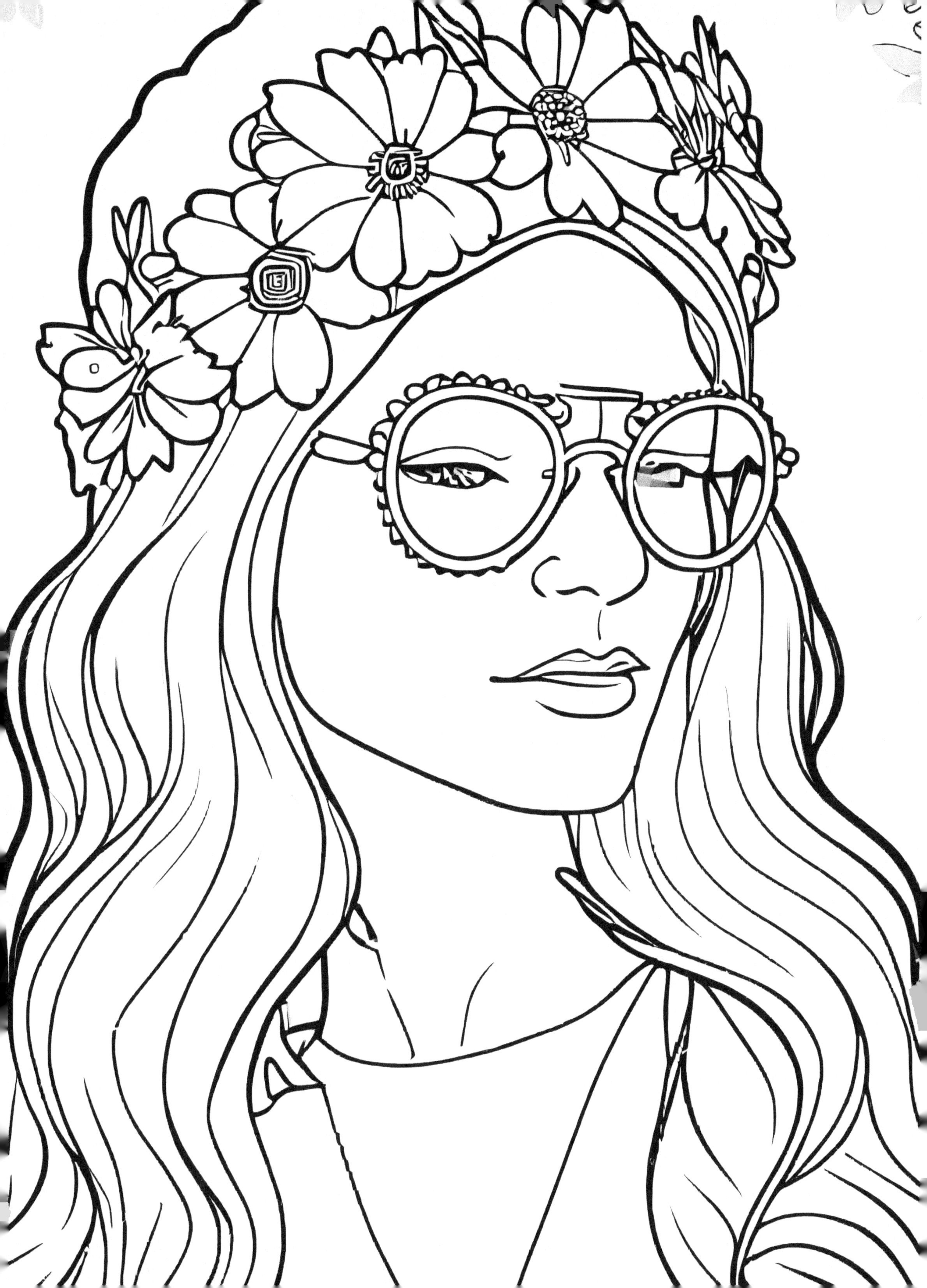

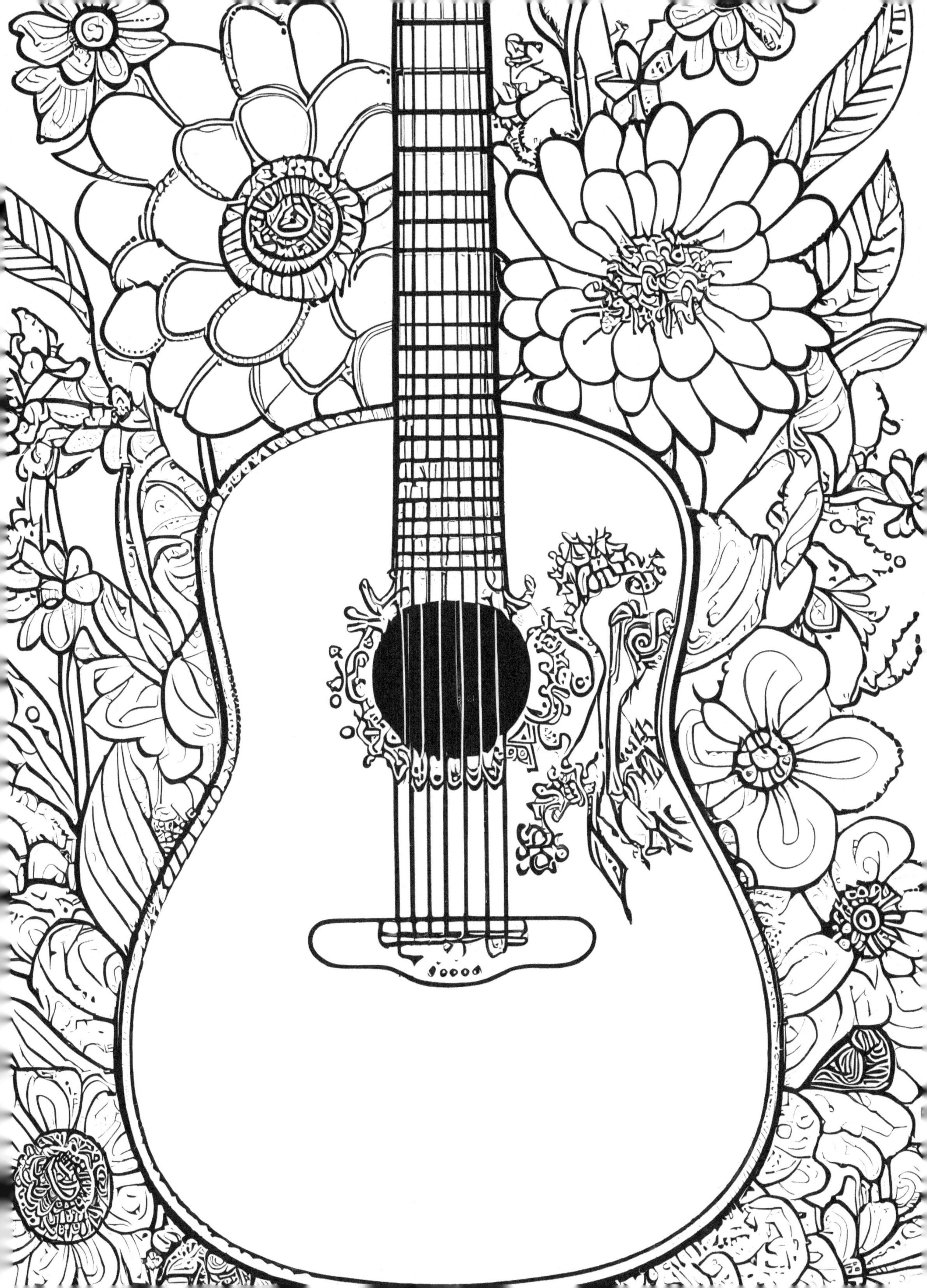

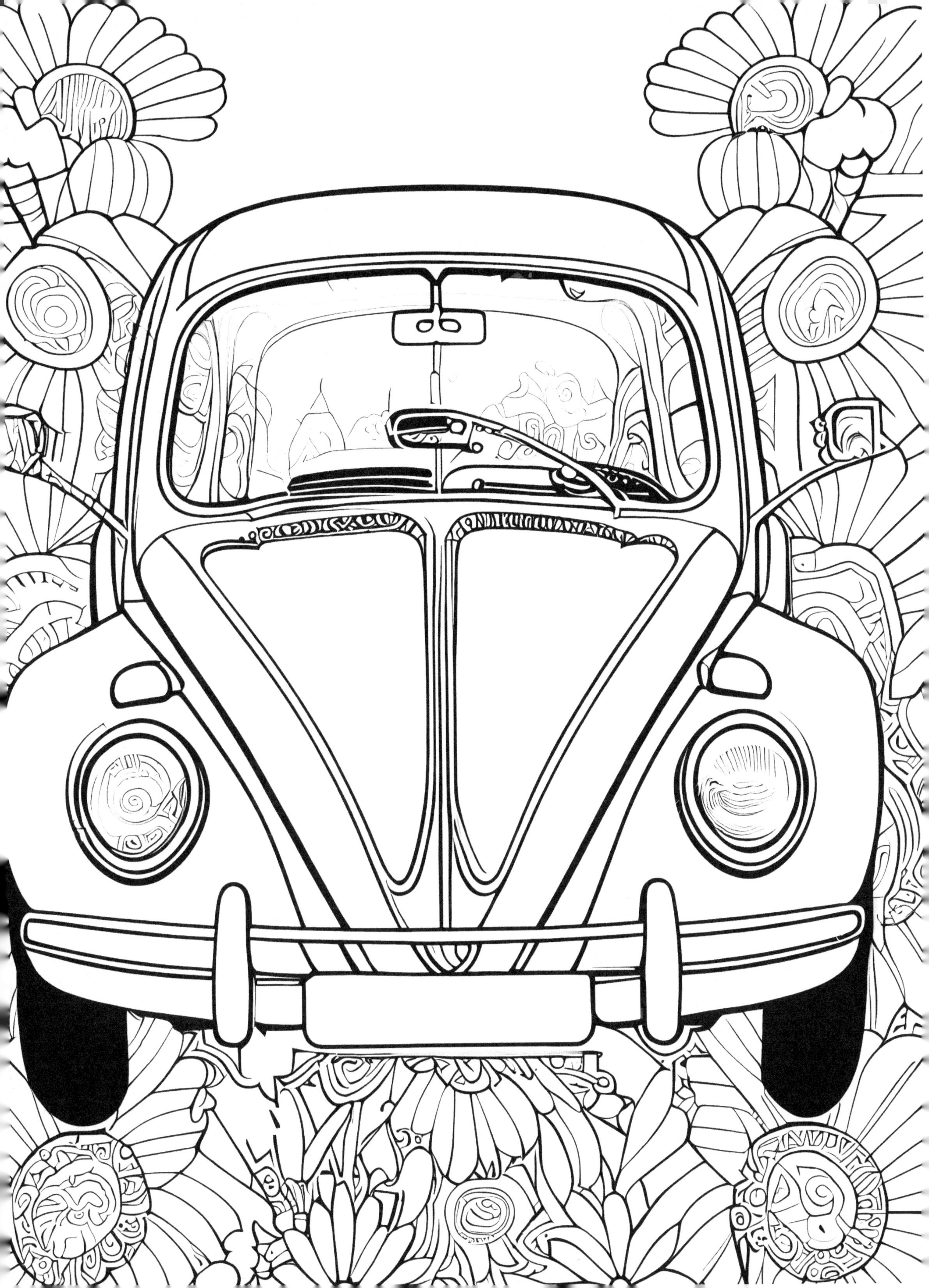

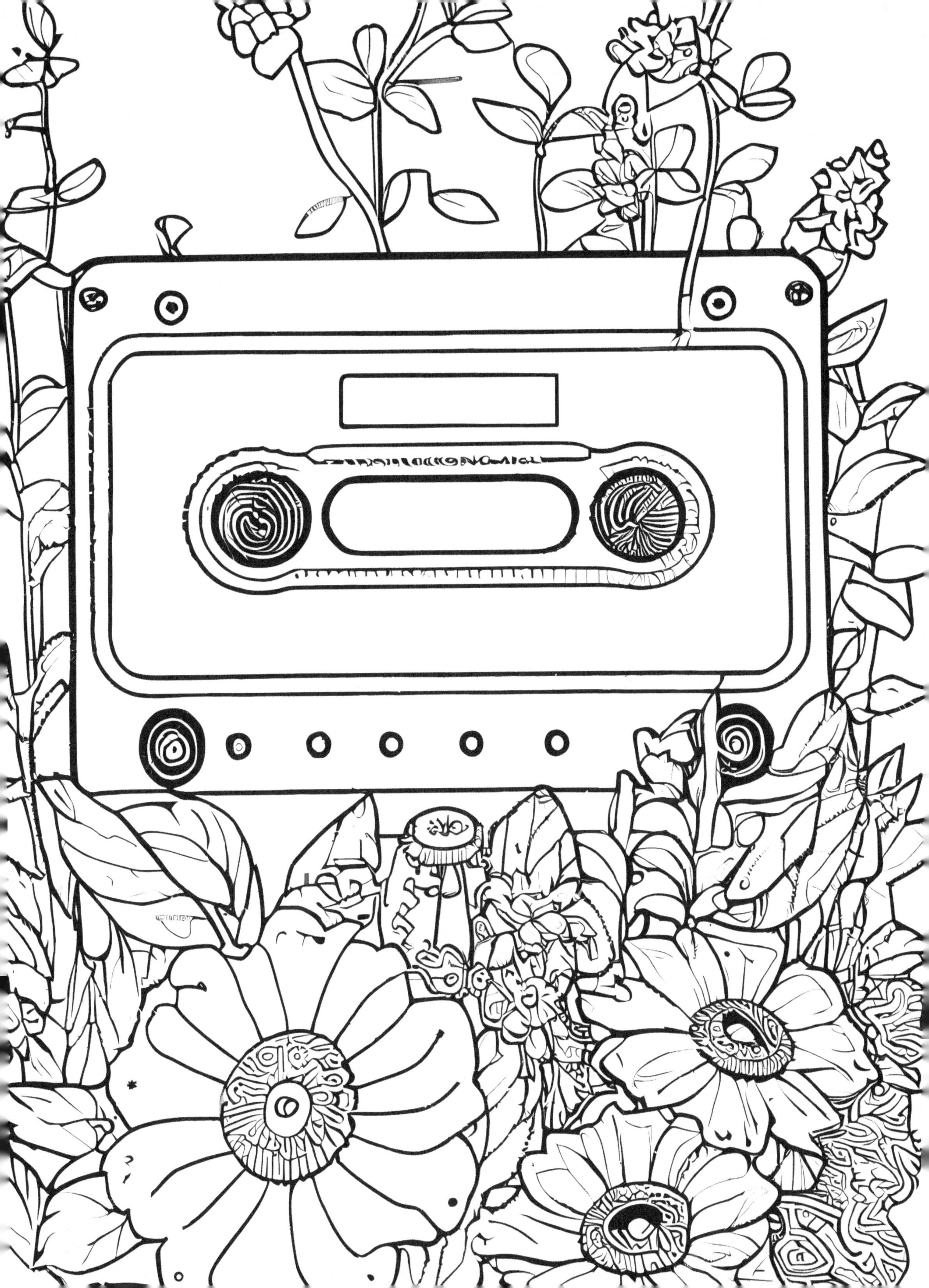

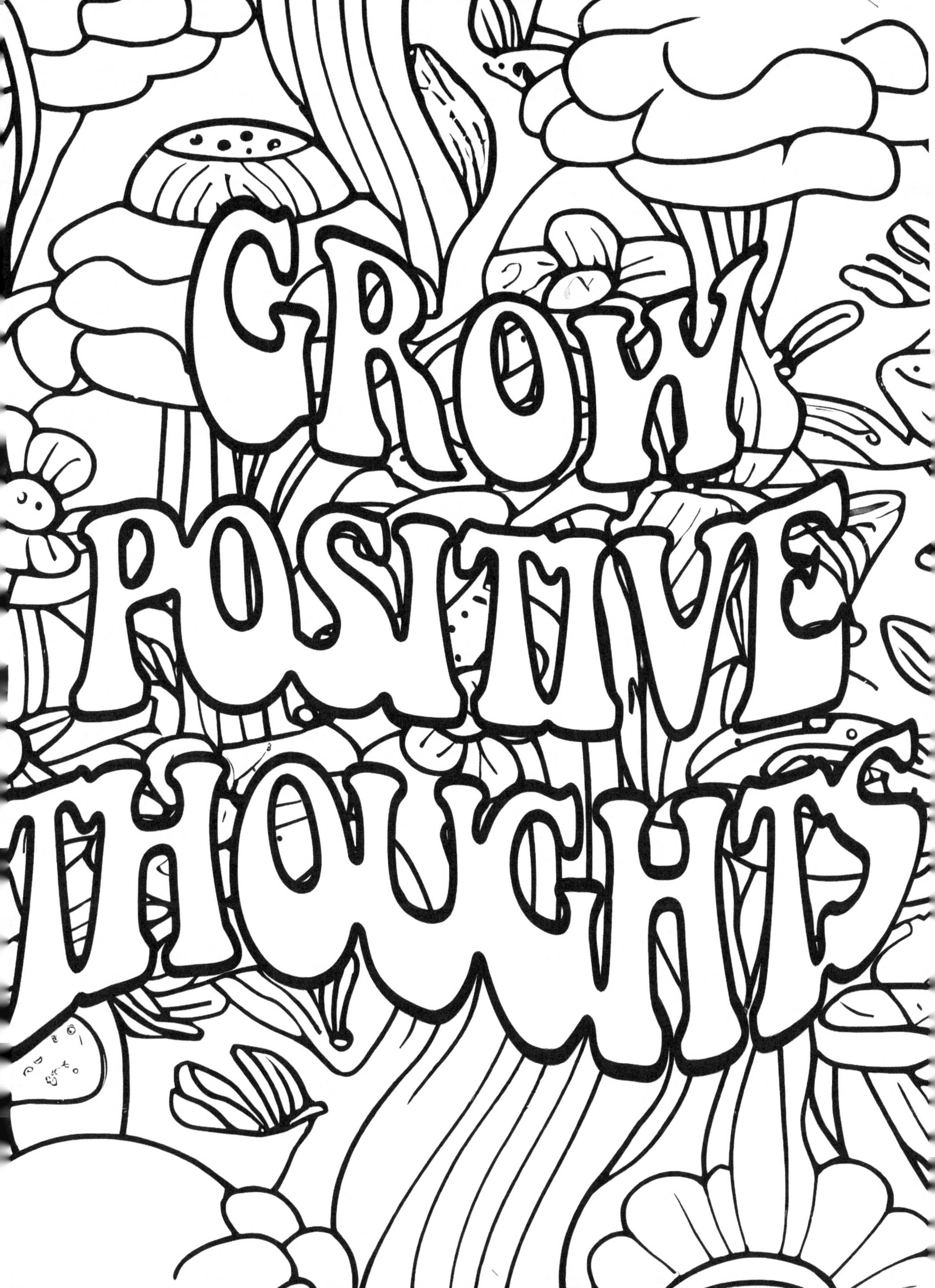

GROW
POSITIVE
THOUGHTS

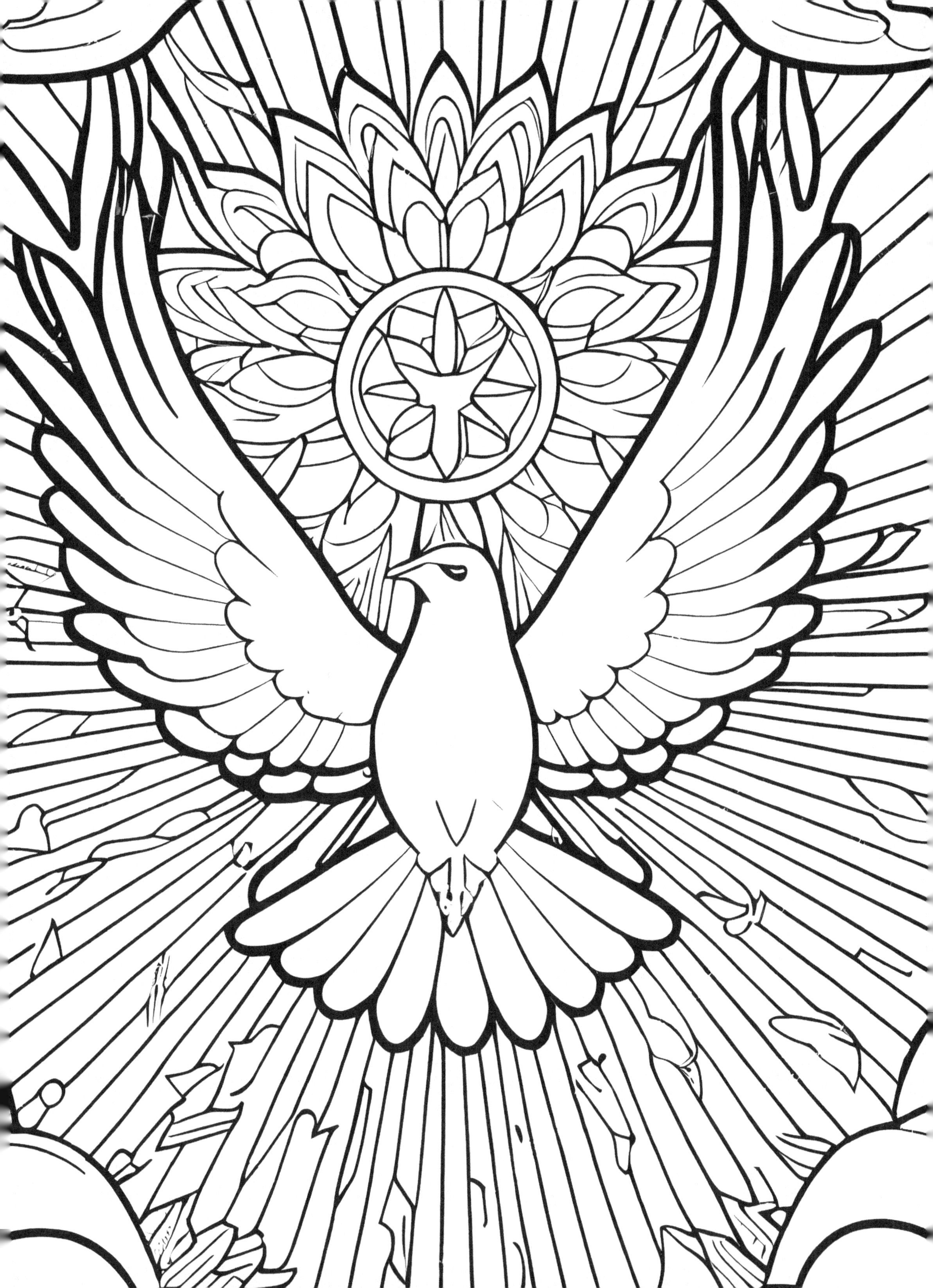

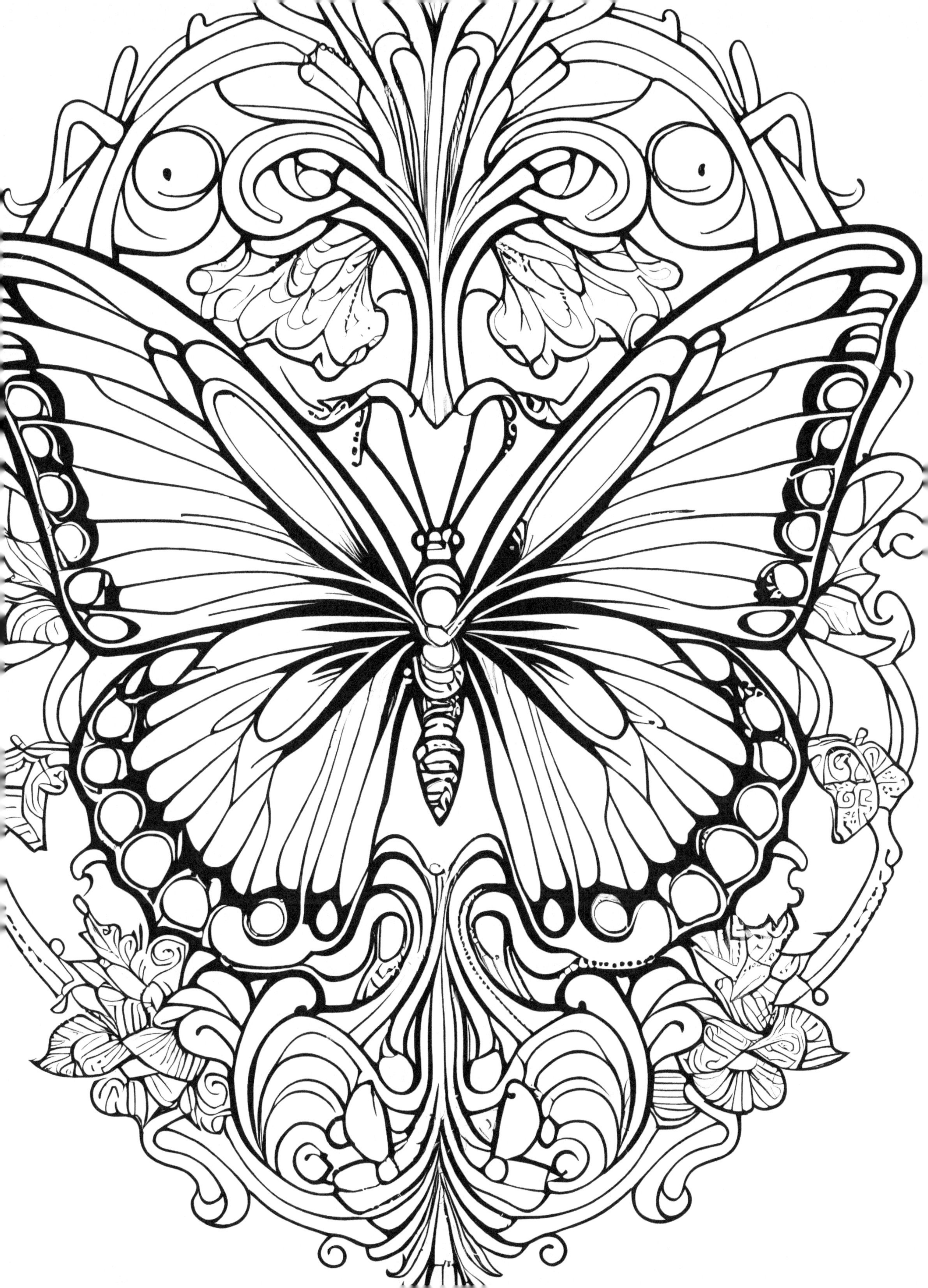

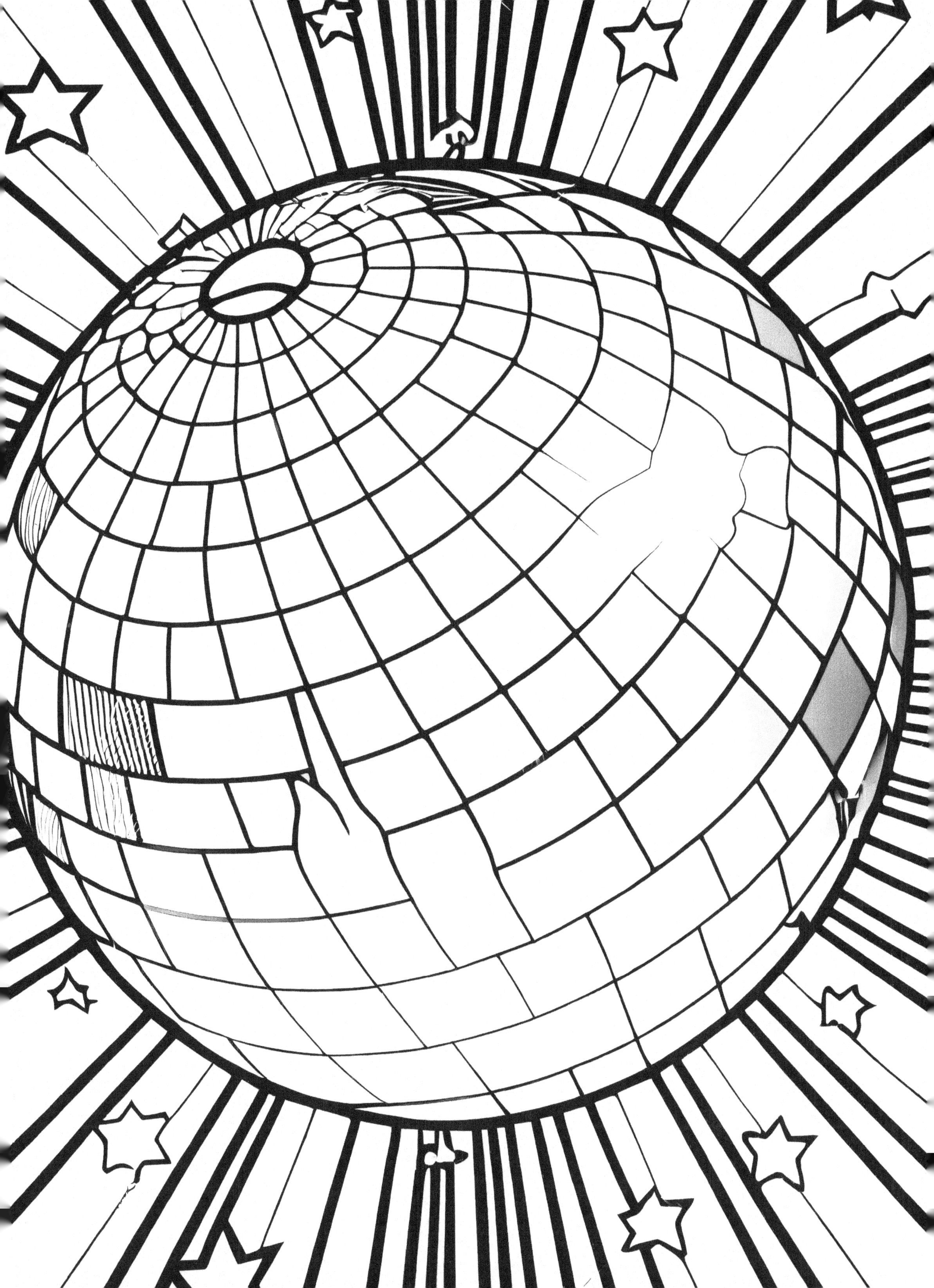

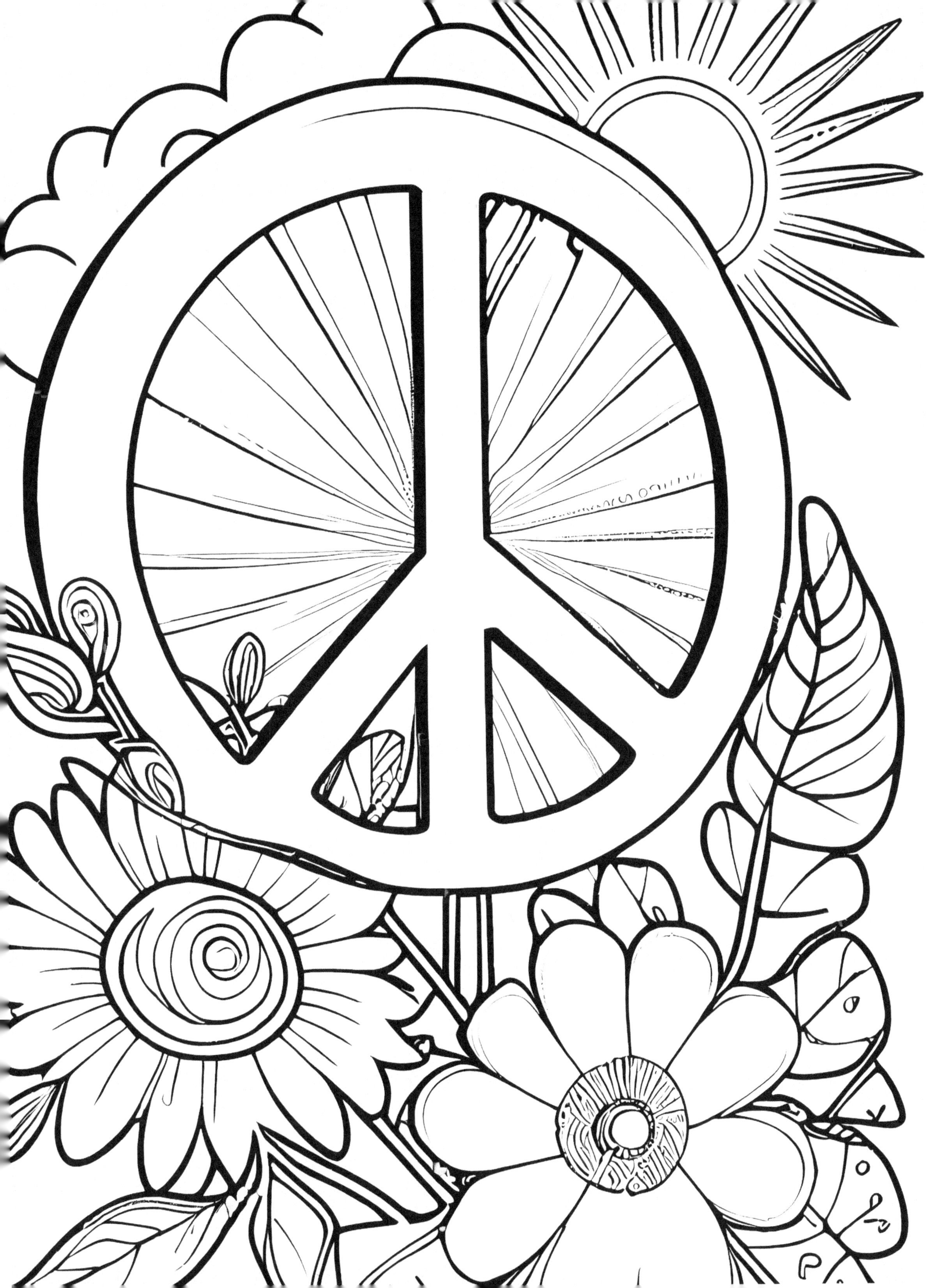

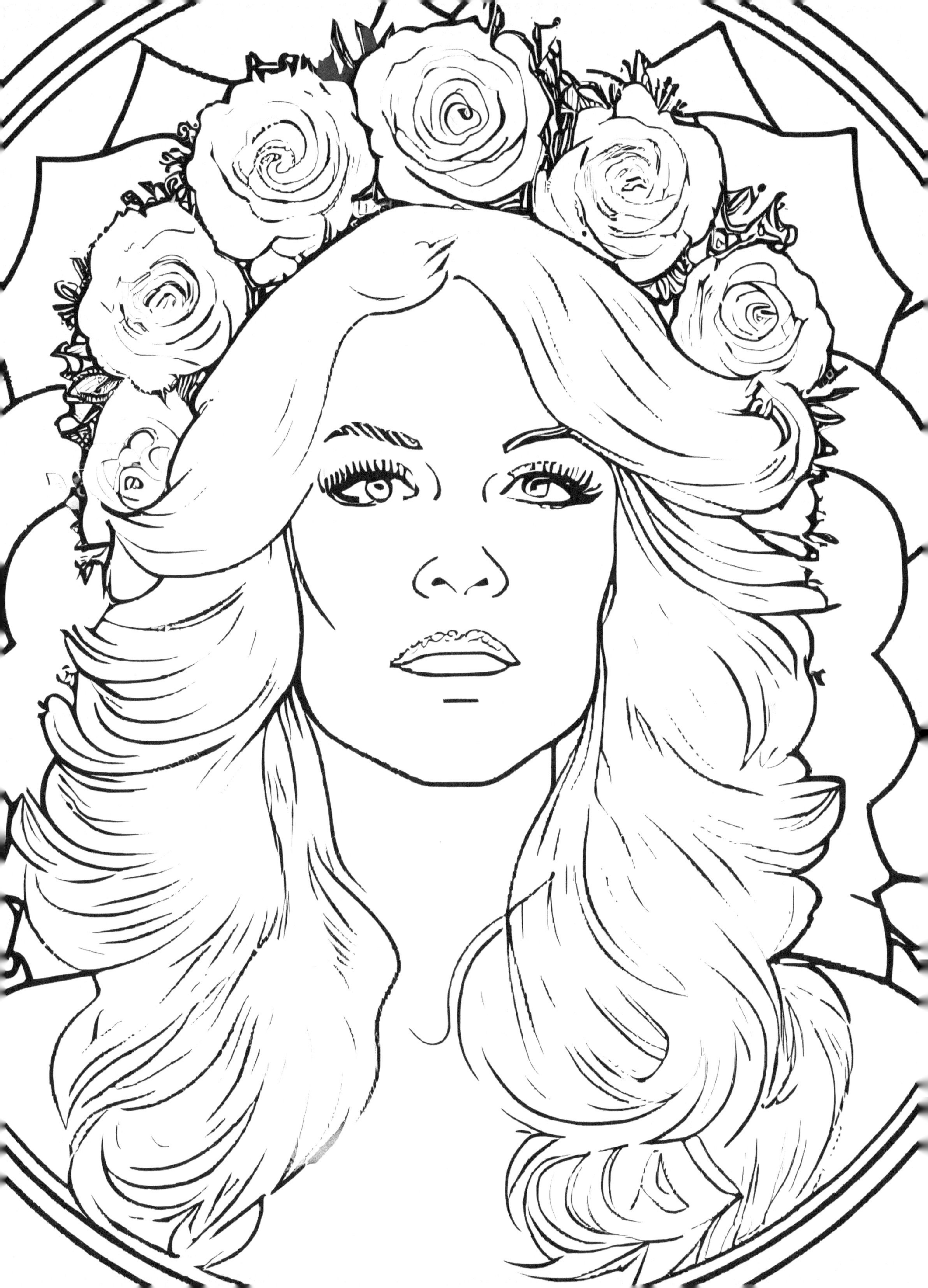

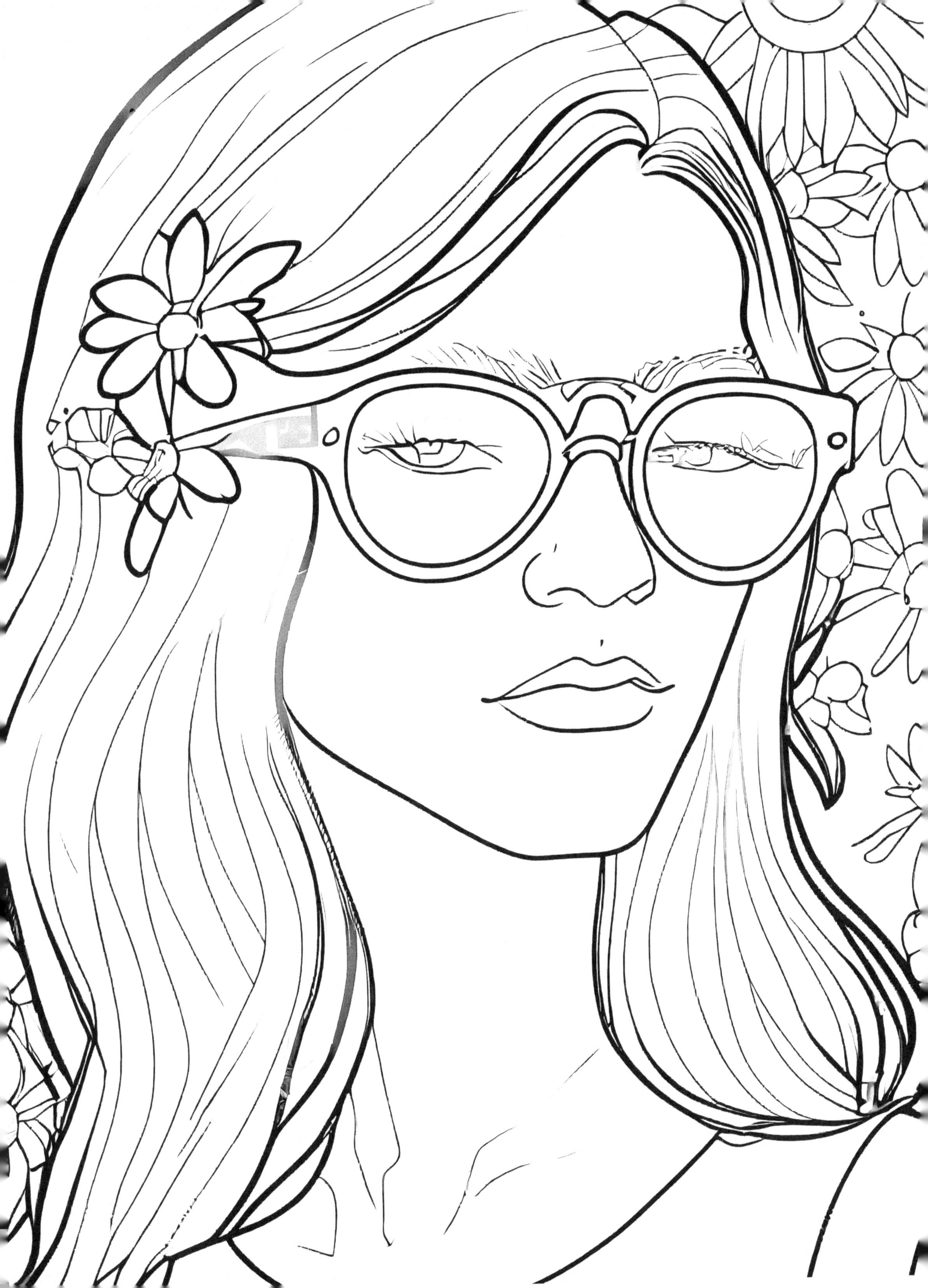

Thank you for colouring your way through
this delightful journey with
Brooks Brotherz colouring books!

We hope you've had a fantastic time
exploring our designs.

Your feedback means the world to us,
and we'd love to hear your thoughts.

If you enjoyed this coloring book,
please consider leaving a review on Amazon
to share your experience with others.

Your reviews help us continue creating
wonderful coloring adventures for everyone
to enjoy.

Thank you for your support,
and happy colouring!

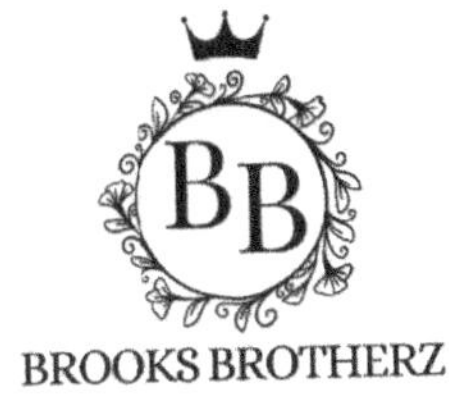

www.ingramcontent.com/pod-product-compliance
Lightning Source LLC
Chambersburg PA
CBHW080917260726
48661CB00009B/3698